THE FAITHFUL SKEPTIC

In Search of a Humble Christianity

THE FAITHFUL SKEPTIC

In Search of a Humble Christianity

†

Jan G. Linn

© 2025 by Jan G. Linn
All Rights Reserved
No part of this book may be reproduced in any form or by any electronic or mechanical means including information storage and retrieval systems without permission in writing from the publisher, except by a reviewer who may quote brief passages in a review.

Sunstone books may be purchased for educational, business, or sales promotional use. For information please write: Special Markets Department, Sunstone Press, P.O. Box 2321, Santa Fe, New Mexico 87504-2321.
Printed on acid-free paper
∞
eBook: 978-1-61139-69-7

Library of Congress Cataloging-in-Publication Data

Names: Linn, Jan author
Title: The faithful skeptic : in search of a humble Christianity / Jan G. Linn.
Description: Santa Fe : Sunstone Press, [2025] | Includes readers guide. | Includes bibliographical references. | Summary: "Being a faithful skeptic holds the key to modern Christianity becoming more humble in admitting it doesn't have all the answers to life's timeless questions but can offer guidance to people knowing the critical questions to ask in their pursuit of truth"-- Provided by publisher.
Identifiers: LCCN 2025012619 | ISBN 9781632937278 paperback | ISBN 9781632937285 hardback | ISBN 9781611397697 epub
Subjects: LCSH: Truth--Religious aspects--Christianity | Skepticism | Faith and reason--Christianity | Humility--Religious aspects--Christianity | Apologetics
Classification: LCC BT50 .L5535 2025 | DDC 230--dc23/eng/20250714

LC record available at https://lccn.loc.gov/2025012619

WWW.SUNSTONEPRESS.COM
SUNSTONE PRESS / POST OFFICE BOX 2321 / SANTA FE, NM 87504-2321 /USA
(505) 988-4418

CONTENTS

1 / Getting on Track † 9
2 / The Necessity of Christian Skepticism † 15
3 / Skepticism and Church Teaching † 21
4 / Making Peace with Science † 29
5 / Reading the Bible Honestly † 39
6 / Remembering Who's on First † 49
7 / Room in the Inn for Jesus † 61
8 / Redundant Salvation † 71
9 / The Breath of Life † 79
10 / The Bible and Culture Wars † 83
11 / Community Rather than Conformity † 93
12 / Working Out Your Own Salvation † 103
13 / The End of Our Days † 111
14 / Christian Skepticism and Hope † 123
15 / The Way Forward † 129
Post-Script for Ministers (and Everyone in Ministry) † 135

Acknowledgments † 143
Notes † 145
Readers Guide † 153

"True religion is not about possessing the truth. No religion does that. It is rather an invitation into a journey that leads one toward the mystery of God. Idolatry is religion pretending that it has all the answers."

—John Shelby Spong[1]

✝

1

GETTING ON TRACK

The 2024 Paris Olympic Games were among the best I have ever seen, and I've lived long enough to see more than a few. They began with a stunning Opening Ceremony conducted on the Seine River that runs through the middle of Paris in a pouring rain. The staff and the athletes deserved the world's gratitude and admiration for not letting the weather spoil anything about the evening. The next day, though, some French Catholic Bishops decided to rain on the already rain-soaked parade of festive boats and shoreline dramatic celebrations by accusing the organizers of having a scene that made fun of the Last Supper as depicted in Leonardo de Vinci's famous painting. American evangelicals quickly joined the bishops in their criticism. One of them, Harrison Butker, NFL place kicker for the Kansas City Chiefs, posted a verse of scripture on X (formerly Twitter) warning the organizers of the Opening Ceremony, "Be not deceived, God is not mocked. For what things a man shall sow, those also shall he reap. For he that soweth in his flesh, of the flesh also shall reap corruption. But he that soweth in the spirit, of the spirit shall reap life everlasting." (KJV) The post received over a million views.[2]

The problem, of course, with all these criticisms was that the scene in question had nothing to do with the Last Supper, but was a re-enactment of a bacchanal or feast to the Greek god Dionysus arriving at the banquet table of the gods of Olympus as an acknowledgement of the Olympic Games beginning in ancient Greece. On several levels these misguided criticisms of the Opening Ceremony were disturbing. Not only did they make Christians look intellectually shallow in displaying such an appalling lack of historical knowledge about the Games. It confirmed once again the image of Christianity as a religion of beliefs that often lead people to make judgmental public statements of others that is rooted in an unconscious self-righteousness.

I decided to write a blog about it, though I confess I didn't expect to get much response. I simply wanted to take exception to this misguided religiosity once again in public view. My modest expectations widely missed the mark. Immediately comments thanking me for the blog began to be posted and in less than an hour over a hundred people had read the blog. Within forty-eight hours more than six-hundred people had read it directly or on Facebook, shared it with others, and before it was over more than eight hundred people had viewed it. Here is the first part of the blog to which most people responded:

> Let me be clear up front. I am Christian, but I am not a Christian and don't ever want to be again, at least in the sense of what that has come to mean today. Being Christian is about how you live. Being a Christian is about what you believe, and what some Christians believe makes Christianity trivial, judgmental, mythological, offensive, and at times downright silly.
>
> The latest protest by the kind of Christians I am talking about over the opening ceremony at the Olympic Games is another in a long line of examples of why I no longer call myself a Christian. This one falls into the category of being just plain silly, almost laughable, except it does immense harm to the image of Christianity itself. The opening ceremony had nothing to do with the Last Supper, and certainly wasn't mocking it, but the reaction of the Christians who say it did shows how theologically shallow they are.

I would not have been surprised had readers reacted to my criticism of the bishops and American evangelicals for what I considered an unjustified moralistic criticism of the Opening Ceremony that was based on a complete misunderstanding of it. What I did not expect was the fact that all the comments were positive and focused on the distinction between being a Christian and being Christian, a distinction I first wrote about in a previous book, *Unbinding Christianity*.[3] At the time some people argued that I was making a distinction without a difference, but apparently there was more of a difference in that distinction than they thought according to the people who read my blog.

The distinction is a short-hand way of highlighting the difference between a Christianity that focuses more on conformity of beliefs than actually living a life based on the life and teachings of Jesus. While we can agree that the two should be one and the same, we know that is not the case. Indeed, the comments on my blog suggested quite clearly that there are Christians today who are ready to respond to an emphasis on the way Christians are supposed to live instead of what Christians are supposed to believe. If the church is going to try to attend to that hunger, though, it will need to teach and preach a Christianity that is more humble about what it knows, honest about what it doesn't, and more willing to listen to people's questions instead of being determined to give them answers.

At its core this book is about the critical need for Christian skeptics who are willing to ask questions before affirming and accepting anything and everything the church says, including what Christians should believe. One of the signs of wisdom as a person of faith is recognizing the indispensable role questions play in arriving at good and sound conclusions. Indeed, my experience has been that the older I have gotten, the more enigmatic life seems, to the point where I have far more questions than answers about everything. A clergy friend now in his nineties (who with his wife suggested the title for this book) has said on numerous occasions that today he resonates more with the plea of the prophet Habakkuk when he wrote, "O Lord, how long shall I cry for help, and you will not listen?" than anything he was taught to believe. He wasn't saying he had lost his faith or that he had abandoned Christianity. He was saying that in his later years he has come to realize more than ever that questions are part of being a person of faith, something he never learned in church, but had to learn on his own.

The truth about Christianity and all other religions is that none of them has the truth, only approximations to it. That is not a bad thing when you understand that faith is less about having the right answers and more about knowing the right questions to ask in pursuit of knowledge and any truth to which it leads. As I will underscore in the pages that follow, everything the church has said or says today, its creedal statements, doctrines, dogmas, and elements of faith come from the minds and hearts of good, but flawed human beings and should be evaluated with that in mind. Human fallibility permeates everything we think, touch, and feel, including the pronouncements of church leaders past and present. People can be as wrong in what they believe as they can be right, making it unreasonable, if not arrogant, to think that the divine/human relationship hangs on human beings having right beliefs. The thesis of this book is that Jesus said less about what his followers were to believe and far more about how they were to live.

This is why skepticism is critical to a healthy Christianity. It refuses to let faith settle for answers that are afraid of the questions they raise. While establishing boundaries for what Christians should believe may have been a necessary work in the first three centuries of the Jesus movement, that no longer meets the needs of today's Christians. Basic beliefs have a place in all religions, including Christianity, but they are nonetheless human expressions about God, not messages from God carved in stone as they were in Cecil B. DeMille's film, "The Ten Commandments." While the church has focused most of its energies teaching people about what they should believe, church members have struggled with knowing what being Christian means and how they can live that way in the face of the issues and problems and pressures of daily life. In the face of the rise of Hitler and Nazism, theologian Dietrich Bonhoeffer framed it this way: "It is becoming increasingly clearer every day that the most urgent problem besetting our Church is this: How can we live the Christian life in the modern world."[4]

The struggle to live Christian is still the challenge. What we see today in American Christianity is the temptation to make beliefs ends in themselves rather than helping Christians live by the teachings of Jesus. Bonhoeffer did not say the urgent need was for Christians to believe what the church said they should believe. He said it was how to live the Christian life in the modern world. Implicit, of course, in his words was the subtle indictment of the church of his day for a hypocrisy that eventually led it to its shocking capitulation to Nazism. That story is a sobering reminder that it is easy to mistake being a Christian for being Christian, choosing religiosity over faithfulness, the consequences of which can be catastrophic.

It is, of course, a problem that has existed from the beginning of the Jesus movement. The Letter of James admonishes the people to whom it was written to be doers of the word instead of hearers only. (1:22) He later reminds them that having faith but no works is useless because a faith that doesn't translate into actions is "a dead faith." (2:14, 17) The core conviction undergirding this book, then, is that Jesus calls Christians to be doers rather than hearers or believers, to live our faith rather than "having" it. It is written to and for Christians who have been turned off by traditional Christianity and dropped out of the church, but haven't given up on Christianity entirely, Christians still in the church, but don't believe much of what the church says they should, and former Christians who pay little attention to the church anymore, but haven't forgotten their spiritual roots. It might even have some appeal to those who have abandoned Christianity completely as they see a version of it that is unafraid of questions, is less burdensome, less judgmental, more circumspect in making claims about itself, and embodies a commitment to justice, kindness, and compassion for others.

In today's America, people attracted to a healthy Christianity are not looking for a message that promotes conformity of belief, but one that is open to questions because it recognizes the value of skepticism in serving as a guide to living well and making the world a better place in the process. The next chapter explains why that is the case.

✝

2

THE NECESSITY OF CHRISTIAN SKEPTICISM

Being a Christian skeptic can have a positive impact on your understanding of Christianity and as a result deepen your commitment to living Christian in the world. Indeed, as you read this book I think you will find that skepticism is an essential tool for anyone to whom being Christian matters.

The dictionary definition of "skeptic" is someone inclined to question or doubt accepted opinions, but there's more to it than that, especially for a Christian skeptic. For one thing, it is a choice you have to make, a serious choice according to Dr. Adam Frank who is professor of astrophysics at the University of Rochester. He describes skeptics as people who are committed "to educating themselves on the subjects they've decided to become skeptical about." He goes on to say they are also willing to change their minds when the evidence warrants it.[5]

Skeptics seek to educate themselves on subjects they've decided to become skeptical about. That needs to be underscored. Being a skeptic begins with a decision to be one. Many Christians choose not to be skeptics because they think skepticism is an enemy of faith. In truth, it is a critical tool for living Christian. It serves as a corrective to the way the human brain actually works. In his provocative book, The Skeptics Guide to the Universe: How to Know What's Real in a World Increasingly Full of Fake,[6] neurologist Steven Novella explains just how amazing the human brain is, including why all of us think what we think and feel what we feel. He begins by noting that not all skepticism is the same, that there are two major types. One is philosophical skepticism that asserts actual knowledge is not possible, leaving us only with perceptions that have no objective verification. A second type is scientific skepticism that begins with doubt, suspicion, or questioning in the pursuit of knowledge, a goal it believes can be achieved. Scientific skepticism fits the Greek word for skeptical (skepsis) which means "an investigation or inquiry" conducted by someone who is looking for truth. In this sense, a skeptic is a person who seeks knowledge in order to know what is true and what is not. It does not refer to someone who is skeptical for the sake of doubting everything.

In the search for truth, it is important to know that everything we examine and conclusions we reach are shaped and influenced by "perception biases" Novella defines as "a complex, highly filtered, and active constructive process" in which our brains are constantly engaged. "We do not passively perceive external stimuli like a camera," he goes on to explain. "This constructive process introduces many possibilities for illusion and misperception."[7]

Think of it this way. If you have ever said, "My mind is playing tricks on me," or told someone, "You're only seeing what you want to see," or, "You can't see what's standing right in front of you," or "What you think I said is not what I said at all," or, the big one, "Perception is reality," as it turns out, they're all true. At least, as Novella says, in the sense that our brains process information in such a way that we are convinced things are the way we believe they are. To us, reality truly is what we perceive it to be when in fact it isn't. It all comes down to our brains functioning as a very sophisticated computer that processes information through biases and fallacies that form our thoughts and feelings.

In addition to our biased perceptions, once we perceive anything it instantly becomes a memory which, as Novella also explains, is far more unreliable than many of us realize. In fact, he says a fundamental fact about memories is that whatever it is we are remembering was not the way we think it was. In his words, "Whenever you find yourself saying, 'I clearly remember...' stop! No, you don't. You have constructed a memory that is likely fused, contaminated, confabulated, personalized, and distorted. And each time you recall that memory you reconstruct it, changing it further."[8]

That is only the beginning of how our brains fool us into believing something is either right or logical when it may be neither. We become ensnared in logical fallacies that lead us to wrong conclusions we are sure are true. That human tendency is exacerbated in people of faith because of the emotional investment we have in what we believe. That makes us more resistant to acknowledging our biases and logical fallacies, if we manage to recognize them in the first place. Confirmation bias, the most common fallacy there is, becomes more resistant to challenge the stronger our emotional attachment to it is. As such, Novella, says, our brain produces a "double whammy" effect. Not only does it reduce the negative emotion of facts conflicting with our identity or beliefs, it induces positive emotions in that part of the brain associated with reward.[9]

Given how the human brain functions, one of the ways Christians today can contribute positively to life in America—and in the world—is to accept the truth that the absolute certainty with which Christianity has always made theological claims is absolutely unjustified and unnecessary. After all, our own faith tradition includes the confession that human beings see things as if seeing a reflection in a dim mirror. (1 Corinthians 13:12) In an ironic way, this personal confession of the Apostle Paul serves as a reminder of why skepticism and religious beliefs work together. People are capable of believing virtually anything, some of which can be fanciful or delusional. Only beliefs that are credible have the potential for making the world a better place, beliefs that are the best conclusions you can reach in an honest pursuit of truth. It doesn't mean they are true beyond all doubt, but they can be affirmed as true beyond a reasonable doubt.

Skepticism exposes opinions for what they often are, claims without evidence or reason, mere assertions hardly worth considering. Everybody is entitled to their opinion because they are easy to come by, don't require any intellectual work, and can be thrown around like a football. Beliefs, on the other hand, are the result of serious examination that skepticism demands in order to separate the superficial from the substantive. More than that, it is precisely because of the hard work involved in skepticism that Christians understand that beliefs are not truth itself, but approximations to it. That is why a Christian skeptic keeps asking questions. The search for truth can never be exhausted.

A Christian skeptic, then, is unwilling to accept faith claims at face value in order to take seriously the necessary questions that must be asked if they are to be trustworthy. Does a belief make sense? Does it demand you to believe something that contradicts reason and logic? Does it increase the chance for peace or support the cause of justice? Does it contribute to compassion or expand the circle of inclusion? These are the kinds of questions a Christian skeptic asks. There are no subjects off limits, no sacred turf to be protected. At the same time, the work of being a Christian skeptic involves significant demands, most especially what psychiatrist Scott Peck said was the most difficult activity human beings have to do—to think.[10]

American journalist and satirist H. L. Mencken is reported to have said that 5% of people think, 10% think they think, and 85% would rather die than think. More satire than fact, his point was that thinking is hard work many people, too many, I suspect, don't want to do. But if you want to be a Christian skeptic, and want to experience all the joy that it can bring to your life, thinking is not an option. It is a necessity. That is especially the case in the divided America of today. Being a thinking Christian can cost you friends and even family relationships because of the kind of superficial Christianity on display in the criticism of the Opening Ceremony of the Olympics. Gay and lesbian children have been sent away from the family dinner table. Transgender kids have been put on the street for being who they are. A couple my wife and I know have a classmate of their son's living with them because his parents made him leave the house when he told them he was transgender. Racially mixed marriages are still considered unacceptable by some people. Advocating for government assistance to the poor is called socialism. Insisting the Communion table doesn't belong to the church, but to God and must include anyone who chooses to come to it can divide a congregation.

Unthinking Christians will often put rigid beliefs above relationships because the church speaks with certainty as if beliefs are easily defined and simple to accept. Christianity needs skeptics to counter that attitude of certainty all too common in the Christian community. Certainty is the opposite of faith. Certainty actually makes faith impossible, even as it leads people to a greater emotional investment in their logical fallacies. The stronger our emotional investment, the stronger our resistance to contrary information becomes. It happens to all of us, not just to people we disagree with or who disagree with us, not just people who don't share our faith or believe what we believe. This is an important point for Christians. The church has convinced many Christians that what the church says to believe is not subject to the kinds of biases that affect other beliefs or that Christians are not prone to logical fallacies everyone else is. This has led to hubris among Christians who have closed their minds to facts and truth different from what they already believe.

This is especially the case for Christians who define their faith by a set of beliefs they consider irrefutable truths. The logical fallacy Novella calls "motivated reasoning," defined as "the biased process we use to defend a position, ideology, or belief we hold with emotional investment" also reinforces this tendency.[11] Motivated reasoning is virtually the same thing as confirmation bias except the former is conscious while the latter is not. Both can and often are at work in Christian circles, as I learned early in life in and from the church where I grew up. What drew me to skepticism was that in spite of the logical fallacies that infect all of us, freedom of thought is still possible, especially in regard to matters of faith. Skepticism helped me see that the fears the church had attached to doubt and questions was and is a red herring, a distraction to hide the church's need for authority and power. The best part of becoming a Christian skeptic is in discovering that being Christian and being skeptical are not mutually exclusive, that skepticism is a tool to be used to strengthen faith, not destroy it. Actually, skepticism holds the key to recognizing the logical fallacies and skewed perceptions that lead people to believe things that make no sense and/or contradict evidence-based facts. Novella calls it "metacognition," or "thinking about thinking" wherein you constantly examine your views and beliefs for their biases in the pursuit of reliable knowledge.

Skepticism is threatening only to Christians who remain

stuck in a Christianity afraid of exploring new paths of thought that come into view when we step off the road we've always travelled. Actually, life is a constant diet of questions, doubts, and challenges to our views and perspectives on just about everything. But the search for knowledge and truth energizes life in general and can do the same in regard to faith. "Always be ready to make your defense to anyone who demands from you an accounting for the hope that is in you," I Peter 3:15 reminds us, "yet do it with gentleness and respect." (3:16a) That is a beautiful description of how a Christian skeptic functions within the Christian community. My own experience is that the fruit of such a life is spiritual freedom and a resilient joy. By the time you finish reading this book, I hope you will discover that is also true for you.

3

SKEPTICISM AND CHURCH TEACHING

My mother lived to be a hundred years old. Her formal education stopped after the eighth grade, but she made herself into a genuine renaissance woman. A sketch artist, a painter, a poet, she read voraciously, loved opera, thought Luciano Pavarotti had a voice only God could have given him, and kept herself abreast of the latest news of the day. Few people knew any of these things about my mother. Instead, they knew her as a wife, mother, good neighbor, and faithful church member.

Mother was the best woman I have ever known, kind, gentle, quiet, compassionate, and, most of all, loving. My father was not gentle or quiet, and did not attend church until late in his life, but he was a loving father and a crusader for economic justice, sacrificing his own health working long hours on behalf of just wages and safe working conditions for the labor union members he represented for thirty years. His example was the source and inspiration for my own social conscience.

Most of the adults I knew growing up were like my own parents. Our neighbors who lived next door and across the street, my mother's sister and her husband who were like second parents to me and my brothers, my hometown pastor who served our church for fifty years and his wife who was the playground director in our neighborhood for thirty-five years, The local drugstore owner who carried people's prescription drug medicine bills as long as necessary, my senior high Sunday School teacher and later my secretary when I was a college chaplain. All them were salt of the earth types, attended church every Sunday. Their theology was traditionally Christian, believing as they did that Jesus died for their sins, that they were going to heaven, and that nothing was more important than getting people who hadn't been baptized saved.

These are the people who taught me how to live, to treat people the way I wanted them to treat me, to lend a hand to anybody in need, to be honest, tell the truth, work hard, get the kind of education they didn't have, make something of myself. The older I've gotten the more I have realized how fortunate I was to have the parents I had, grow up in the neighborhood I did, go to the church I attended, have the friends I had as a kid. And, yet, these same people went along with racial segregation as if it were a normal thing to do, as if nothing they heard in church made them question white superiority or discrimination against people simply because of the color of their skin.

If I am honest, I have to say that every adult I knew growing up, including my parents, was unwittingly complicit in southern racism, primarily by not openly questioning the segregated culture in which they lived. Neither my oldest living brother nor I remember our parents using the "N" word in our home, or talking about Martin Luther King, Jr. being the communist agitator the hometown newspaper said he was. But neither did they criticize the "separate but equal" policy of our state government that maintained racial segregation and white privilege.

How did they (and all the others) not connect the dots between being Christian and racial justice? How did our minister's wife who worked with and loved hundreds of poor kids over many years as their playground director oppose integration because she feared it would result in racial inter-marriage she believed would create a "mulatto" race. Everything I needed to know about how to be a good person I learned from people who attended church regularly, and at the same time everything I should have learned from them about racial justice I didn't.

There is, of course, a long and sordid history behind the racism I witnessed during my childhood years. Slavery has been called America's original sin, but Christians were among the last to realize it. At the time they spoke out of both sides of their mouth. While Henry Ward Beecher, famed pastor of Plymouth Congregational Church in New York City was speaking against slavery forcefully four years before the Civil War, at the very same time the South's most prominent preacher, James Henley Thornwell, was telling his Presbyterian congregation in Columbia, South Carolina that slavery was a good and merciful way to organize labor.[12] It was a minister named William Joseph Simmons who re-established the Ku Klux Klan in 1915, made himself its second Imperial Wizard, and designed the hooded cloaks and created the secret rituals the members observed at their meetings, all in the service of what he believed was biblical teaching.

A hundred years later the children and grandchildren of these Christians also failed to see the sin of slavery even after our nation fought and won a war against itself to end it. Instead, they supported a different form of slavery called state sanctioned segregation. Once again Christians chose to be "representative" of their age instead of citizens of God's kingdom on earth.[13] It was only when the black church lead a civil rights movement that challenged segregation and exposed the racism it represented that a significant number of white Christians and their churches began to choose racial justice over white supremacy. But it was a painstakingly slow process. I came into ministry at this time and was immediately confronted with a Christianity in the church too weak and compromised to speak truth to power or any truth at all. It was a hard, but invaluable lesson to learn through bitter experience that preaching the gospel and social justice could not be separated, and certainly not segregated, and remain Christian.

Yet, the struggle continues. The failure of Christians to connect the dots between Christianity and justice in all its manifestations has been a persistent dilemma. Gay and lesbian Christians continue to be judged and excluded by churches and individuals as if they are unworthy of respect or being loved for who they are. Women continue to be treated in many Christian circles as subservient to men, often justified by the faux platitude that discrimination against them is the church's way of honoring the special role in life God has given them. Today Christians who have managed largely on their own to connect their faith with their attitudes and behavior wonder if the church will ever see that how it acts often contradicts the message of love it preaches.

If you grew up in a church, you can know what you learned about racial justice (or any other issue of justice), by asking yourself, "When did I first become aware of racism?" or, "From whom did I learn that judging people on the basis of the color of their skin was wrong?" You may not remember those years clearly, but the one thing every Christian should have in common is remembering that one of the places they learned about racism was in their church. Yet, in a recent conversation with twenty older adults all of whom were raised in the church, not one of them remembered that being the case for them.

The church is often quick to point out the moral weaknesses of individuals while speaking as if its own declarations have not been filtered through that same flawed humanness. It is quick to point to individual failings and sin, but seldom, if ever, admits to its own failings and sins as an institution. While the reason the adults in my life growing up failed to connect the teachings of Jesus with racial justice may have been solely their own, more likely is that they believed a church that itself failed to make that connection. As true as it is that Christians never stop being human beings with the weaknesses, flaws, mistakes and errors of judgment endemic to the human condition, neither does the church.

Why is an enigma because church leaders know how flawed both they and the church are. I remember the late United Methodist Gerald Kennedy telling the story of a man who came to visit him and spent the entire time complaining about how bad the Methodist Church was. He was well informed, giving specific examples Bishop Kennedy also knew about. When the man was finished, Kennedy thanked him for his candor and taking the time to talk. When he left, Bishop Kennedy sat down in his chair, looked out the window behind his desk, and said to himself, "Thank God, he doesn't know any more than he does."

The church is no better than the leadership it has, and those of us who serve in that capacity know the truth about ourselves. It is easy for us to forget or ignore that before we were ever ministers, we were human beings, flawed as all people are. That is why church teaching doesn't come from God and never has. It comes from flawed human beings, mostly men. The fact that for centuries these "men" of God excluded women from clergy leadership, and in many instances still do, proves just how flawed they are.

It is past time for the church to admit its own humanness. The church can be an important voice in society without being infallible. The way to be better is not to pretend it isn't flawed, but to become more humble about itself. Hypocrisy cannot exist when humility is real, and humility depends on self-honesty. A strong church is one that is unafraid to tell the truth about itself. We live at a time when the church's insistence that it speaks with authority given to it by God needs to be tempered by honesty about its humanness. It may speak of what it believes to be the will of God, but that is not at all the same thing as it being the will of God. I believe the church has and still does teach and preach what it believes is the will of God, but it needs more humility as it does. The reality of the humanness of those who lead the church demands it. There doesn't need to be a perfect gospel or a perfect proclamation of it for it to be credible and winsome. It, instead, needs to be honest. That will be enough to give it authority without being resistant to questions skeptics not only will ask, but must ask in their pursuit of a place to stand within the Christian tradition.

When a clergy friend of mine was a boy there were four churches in the small town where he grew up, three Protestant and one Catholic. He belonged to one, but he attended all four because of having friends in each one. One day he told his mother that he was troubled by something negative the minister of one of the churches said about the other three. His mother immediately responded, "Well, Don, you don't have to believe everything you hear in church."

Not everyone is fortunate enough to have a wise mother like that. Not everyone who attends church is fortunate enough to have a wise minister like his mother, or wise church members. Most of us grew up being told we needed to believe everything we heard in church. Many ministers and churches still tell people that, as if what the church teaches and preaches is not open to debate. It is to be accepted at face value, either because it's official church teaching, as in the case of Catholics, or because it's what the Bible says, as in the case of Protestants. But the counsel of my friend's mother is wiser. You don't have to believe everything you hear in church. In fact, once you commit yourself to showing love for God by loving your neighbor as you love yourself, you don't need to believe anything unless and until you have examined it for yourself to see the truth of it.

The reason lies, as I have been saying, in our humanity. Everything we believe is the result of willful and unwitting biases that influence and shape how we process information that informs what we believe, think, and feel, including Christianity. It can't be any other way because it's the way our brains work. Everything everyone, including Christians, thinks, believes, and understands is biased by who they are. Each of us is an interpretative context through which we process information. That is why the truth we believe and believe in is unavoidably subjective. Given the nature of beliefs, the best we can hope for is to make approximations to truth. Nothing we believe is objective truth. If it were it would no longer be a belief, but a fact.

Beliefs are always and unavoidably the result of who we are, our gender, race, age, knowledge, family relationships, church backgrounds, personal experiences because that is how our brains function. Sometimes beliefs are little more than an extension of what someone else has told us to believe. Beliefs can reflect significant insights into a subject or they can hinder a better understanding of it. Some beliefs assist us in the pursuit of truth while others get in the way. It's important that we know which is which by monitoring ourselves to minimize the effect of biases. Unfortunately, the church has not done that. Its history is one of declaring truths and beliefs and doctrines and dogma as if they come from God instead of the minds of human beings who are not God and seldom godly.

The church doesn't need what it says to be labeled with divine sanction to speak with authority. The more church teaching appears to justify itself as if it has the truth, the whole truth, and nothing but the truth, the less authority it has because people know that is not true. The church is a human institution that speaks about God as best it can, but a Christian skeptic knows it doesn't speak for God. Never has and never will. The church should know that by now. It should know that when it speaks, people don't listen unless what it says connects with something deep inside they already know is true. All religious claims are subject to the nuances endemic to being human. They may be brilliant, insightful, helpful, even inspiring. They may be none of these. They may make sense when held up to scrutiny or they may contradict common sense.

In the context of faith, being a skeptic is not about doubting everything and refusing to believe anything. It is about asking the right questions to get as close to truth as possible and also beyond it to a different kind of truth that is related to the meaning and purpose of life. Skepticism is a way for the church to show maturity, knowing questions move people forward while blind acceptance of what is taught and claimed to be true risks being left behind. The church has often been its own worst enemy, making declarations about what to believe as if not to believe them disqualified you from being Christian.

I became a Christian skeptic when I first realized that I needed to unlearn most of what I had been taught in church. When I began my theological studies, I remember wondering why I had never heard any of it before, especially since what I was learning helped the message of Jesus make more sense than anything the church had taught me. Church history tells the story of Christian beliefs being unavoidably fluid, evolving, dynamic. My own journey has been one of moving from a faith set in stone to one that is open-minded and marked by a search for knowledge and information that can make it big enough for a world that has grown increasingly smaller. Faith is, of course, more than knowledge because it involves beliefs that transcend the rational, that embrace the reality of mystery. Even then, an open mind is essential to avoiding going down the rabbit hole of conspiracy theories and mistaking myth for history.

The gift of being a skeptic is the key to not giving up on Christianity. It may be that there will also come a time again when Christians will find a place in a church that has learned from its mistakes and is committed to creating communities where questions are welcomed and answers are open to new thoughts and insights. I am grateful I have spent my life in the church while knowing that getting to where I am today spiritually, which is the best place I have ever been, has often been in spite of the church rather than because of it. Perhaps what I have written here will help you find this to be true for yourself. Being a skeptic is not something to overcome. Just the opposite. It is the best way to find your own path to a way of life that allows you to stand on solid ground, not in spite of the questions you have, but because of them.

4

MAKING PEACE WITH SCIENCE

Once I finished the first draft of this book, I asked a former college faculty colleague to read it. Now retired, I knew his evaluation would be grounded in the sciences, chemistry being his field of study, and because we knew each other well I could also trust that he would be candid in whatever he had to say. He graciously agreed, but added that he first wanted me to know his current views on religion. He then sent me some personal reflections he had recently written about his journey from being raised in the church, serving as an active lay leader for many years, and then later in life choosing to give up believing in God and leave both the church and Christianity. I was so impressed by what he said that I asked him for permission to share it here. In part, this is what he said:

> I've been enormously fortunate to have suffered no real trauma in my life. I came from a stable family in comfortable circumstances, my parents were well-educated and saw that I was. I was gifted with academic talent that let me become what my dad was—a college professor. I was smarter than I remember when I met and married my wife, and we were gifted with two healthy and happy and decent children. I tell you this not to boast—all the merit I can claim is that I didn't waste the opportunities handed to me on a silver platter—but to make the point that where I have wound up philosophically is because this is where I have reasoned myself to, not because I have had something bad happen to me and felt the need to make sense of it.

I was almost literally raised in the Southern Baptist Church, in East Texas for the first nine years of my life, and then in Southwest Arkansas until I left for graduate school. In my childhood it was a theologically conservative church but not necessarily fundamentalist. My parents certainly weren't fundamentalists. I remember my dad shaking his head at someone in his Sunday School class who according to my dad "apparently believes God dictated the Bible in King James English." Our church was where most of faculty and staff of the Southern Baptist college in town attended. PhDs might be crazy (and many are), but they (usually) aren't stupid. So, conservative but generally thoughtful. Baptists did several things for me for which I will always be grateful, and the main one was to instill an appreciation for the Bible, for reading it and trying to understand it, for taking it seriously but not necessarily literally. In so doing they perhaps sewed seeds unintentionally, because it led me to a lifelong study of the origins of the Bible, its various canonical texts, what got excluded, what agendas various writers had, how Jewish "theology" evolved over centuries. And that led me to views rather different from some of what I was taught.

In graduate school I was too busy to mess with church until I met my wife who had been raised a Methodist. She made it clear she was not going to join a Baptist church. Marriage is one of the strongest forces for conversion, or at least for denomination switching. But as I studied the Methodists, I found myself attracted to their ideas.

So I immersed myself in the Methodist church, serving on every committee known to man. I joked to one of my pastors that I must have "committee chair" stamped on my forehead. But over time, I began to move farther and farther away from orthodox Christianity, especially from the dogma and theology, from the things you are supposed to believe as opposed to the ways you are supposed to act. For me, there was no blinding flash of light, no Damascus Road experience, no big single event that represented a sharp break with the past. It was quite gradual.

Did my scientific training play a part in this, in rejecting ideas for which I saw no evidence? Undoubtedly. But then my temperament and tendencies—my neurochemical wiring—is one that attracted me to science anyway. My training just reinforced and gave structure to the way my thinking runs.

Why did I stay in the church so long when I no longer believed the things you are supposed to believe to call yourself a Christian? There was the social aspect—there were and are people there I really enjoyed being around. I stayed because of pastors I loved and admired. I stayed because it was a means for doing good, for supporting local nonprofits helping the less fortunate, and the church gave me a point of connection to that. And in the last few years I stayed because I wanted to be in a position of leadership to influence church law concerning the treatment of LGBTQ people.

So what is my philosophical position? I am neither spiritual nor religious. I hope I am ethical. I am too deeply steeped in Biblical traditions to avoid pulling up a Bible verse from memory to explain an idea or to illustrate a point, but the ideas and positions are ethical ones, not theological ones. Theology frankly makes little sense to me. I am a strict materialist, in that I believe the reality accessed through our senses, and through instruments that enhance our senses, is all the reality there is.

I share his story for two reasons. One is that it illustrates something very important for Christians and all people of faith to understand, which is that people who reject the reality of God can be and usually are good people whose values make the world better. Nor are they necessarily anti-religion. The second is that a scientist may reject believing in God for reasons other than conclusions to which science has led them. In other words, both scientists who embrace the concept of God and those who don't can still agree that science does not necessarily make believing in God impossible. Hold that thought as we get further into this discussion.

Let's begin, though, with the fact that religion and science have been at odds for centuries, in large measure because one of the mistakes early Christians leaders made was declaring war on science. Not consciously, but that was de facto what they did when they insisted their religious beliefs trumped the nascent field of scientific discovery. They believed the Bible said the earth was flat, the sun rotated around the earth, and they lived in a three-story universe where heaven and hell were spatial realities. They knew nothing about gravity, about falling stars, galaxies, or anything else we know today about the universe. In the 19th century the church condemned an English biologist named Charles Darwin for his theory of evolutionary biological development through natural selection.

Quite unintentionally these Christian leaders managed to position the church in a no-win situation that continues today. When religion fights with science, it always loses. I don't know if church leaders originally intended to start a war with science, but that became their legacy. It is likely that they simply didn't know what they were doing. They articulated the way they understood their world as if they actually did. It took only a short period of time for science to prove they didn't, but their response was to fight harder, eventually codifying their views into doctrine and dogma and official teachings that turned the conflict with science into a willful act. The result was a Christianity that gained the reputation for instilling a fear of science into all Christians from which modern Christianity has never fully recovered. In the process they also proved that when religion becomes an adversary of science, it not only loses the argument, it loses credibility.

But fault lies on both sides of the conflict. Some scientists hold anti-religious views no less adamant than the anti-scientific views of the church. In the modern era, the New Atheists movement of the late 20th century widely promoted its core belief that there is no supernatural or divine reality and that religion is nothing more than superstition that is fundamentally non-rational, if not altogether irrational. Its primary voices were the late writer Christopher Hitchens, scientists Richard Dawkins, and philosophers Sam Harris and Daniel Dennett. By the beginning of this century they were convinced the days of religious devotion were numbered as more and more people realized humans had created God rather than the other way around. Dawkins argues that religion (meaning "Christianity") hasn't disappeared because it is a meme virus that keeps spreading like a parasite of the brain.[14] A meme, a word he created, is an idea, style, or behavior that spreads within human culture, even to the point of becoming dangerous,[15] which is how Dawkins sees religion.

As Mark Twain said in a cable he sent from London to the press in the U. S. after his obituary had been mistakenly published, "Reports of my death are greatly exaggerated,"[16] so we might say the same thing regarding the reports by the New Atheists of the death of religion. At the same time, Creationism which promotes an anti-scientific world-view provides New Atheism with ample evidence it needs to argue that Christianity is hopelessly anti-science. Creationists have not been deterred. They have established the Creation Museum in Petersburg, Kentucky in 2007 that promotes a chronological story of creation based on the pseudo-scientific young earth theory that insist the earth is only 6,000 years old. A sister museum located 40 miles away in Williamsburg, Kentucky is the Ark Museum that features a giant replica of Noah's Ark.

It is precisely this kind of anti-scientific attitude that is held by a small number of Christians that feeds the public perception that being Christian requires you to believe in nonsense. It doesn't. There is a more balanced and spiritually healthy view of science and religion that refuses to accept the argument that they are incompatible world views. Instead, they ask entirely different questions in search of entirely different answers that do not clash or contradict one another. It's a view held by numerous world renown scientists such as Albert Einstein who suggested that science and religion should not be in conflict. "Science without religion is lame," he famously said, "and religion without science is blind."[17] Though not one who believed in a personal God, Einstein was clear that the conflict between science and religion was not only unnecessary, but impossible, explaining:

If one conceives of religion and science according to these definitions then a conflict between them appears impossible. For science can only ascertain what is, but not what should be, and outside of its domain value judgments of all kinds remain necessary. Religion, on the other hand, deals only with evaluations of human thought and action: it cannot justifiably speak of facts and relationships between facts. According to this interpretation the well-known conflicts between religion and science in the past must all be ascribed to a misapprehension of the situation which has been described.[18]

In an article entitled, "When Science and Religion Collide or Why Einstein Wasn't an Atheist," published in Mother Jones, Gordy Slack reports some of the comments by numerous scientists in interviews conducted by the Center for Theology and the Natural Sciences on religion and science. Francisco J. Ayala, for example, a professor of genetics and evolutionary biology at the University of California at Irvine and an ordained Catholic priest, said, "In terms of fulfilling the human spirit, there is a lot to be said about the world, whether it is the physical world or the living world, that is completely outside the realm of science. Science and religion are dealing with different dimensions of reality, different levels of experience. Anybody who thinks that everything in the world can be explained in a reductionistic, materialistic way is just naïve."[19]

Kenneth S. Kendler, a professor of psychiatry and human genetics at Virginia Commonwealth University College of Medicine, admits that he struggles with mixing his religion (Judaism) and his science, even as they have different foundations. "The two," he says, "don't use similar methods, don't have similar goals, and in some substantial ways don't conform to one another. Maybe the best way to put it is to say that they complement one another. They really don't conflict, but they don't entirely exist on the same plane. Knowledge is something that is ultimately testable—wisdom comes in many varieties."[20]

Carl Feit, an Orthodox Jew and professor of biology at

Yeshiva University, said that science is itself a spiritual practice. Invoking Maimonides, the 12th-century Jewish philosopher, physician, scientist, and rabbi, Feit explained:

> The best way to develop a love and appreciation for God is by studying the works of his hand. There are certain blessings that a religious Jew makes every day. Some of them have to do with the fact that the sun rises and sets regularly, that all of the stars travel in their right orbits, and that all of our physiological functions work appropriately. With my knowledge of human physiology, I have a very different, and I think enhanced, appreciation when I make that blessing in the morning.[21]

Slack also quotes the late Lindon J. Eaves, an Anglican priest and professor of human genetics and psychiatry, also at the Virginia Commonwealth University School of Medicine, who said, "There's a large degree of identity between the love of God and the love of truth. And the same kind of rules and passions that we bring to the issue of loving God, the scientist embodies in his passion for truth."[22]

The Slack article is more than 25 years old, but the views expressed by these scientists reflect those still held by many scientists today. According to research reported in "Secularity and Science: What Scientists Around the World Really Think About Religion,"[23] Brandon Vaidyanathan, associate professor and chair of sociology at The Catholic University of America and one of the authors, noted that while the common myth, largely a creation of the West, is that science and religion are in conflict, only 29% of U. S. scientists believe that is the case. "It appears," he says, "that most scientists really are not hostile to religion. In fact, on a global scale, we found that a significant portion of scientists can be characterized as having religious identities, practices or beliefs, and nontrivial proportions say they have 'no doubt' that God exists."[24]

Others agree. Much of the public perception that religion and science are in an inevitable conflict stems from a misreading of the actual situation, according to Rice University sociologist

Elaine Howard Ecklund: "After four years of research, at least one thing became clear. Much of what we believe about the faith lives of elite scientists is wrong. The 'insurmountable hostility' between science and religion is a caricature, a thought-cliché, perhaps useful as a satire on groupthink, but hardly representative of reality."[25]

My own reading of the material has led me to the conclusion that there is middle ground today between science and religion occupied by both scientists and theologians who consider both important and distinctive in what they are about and, therefore, in conflict only when the lines between their different purposes are blurred. They argue for respect on both sides based on the fact that science asks "what" questions and religion asks "why" questions.

Not only is this view the way to Christianity making peace with science, it also provides a genuine basis for ethical principles to serve as a guide in the use of science. Because science enables human beings to do or invent things doesn't mean they should. One of America's most respected clergy and leader in the anti-nuclear weapons movement, William Sloan Coffin, said on numerous occasions that while we humans now have the power to destroy the planet, we don't have the authority to do so. As theologians, Christians must insist that ethics have a voice in discussions about the role and power of scientific development, most especially now that we live in an AI world in which our capacity to distinguish between real and artificial intelligence is being increasingly challenged.

Surveys suggest we have a long way to go to bring the public up to speed in the necessary interplay between science and religion. In a 2020 Pew Research report, 55% said that in general they believe science and religion were in conflict, but only 38% said their personal religious beliefs sometimes conflict with science.[26] Probably several factors account for the difference in the percentages, one of which may be that on a personal level people have discovered that questions science raises about religious beliefs doesn't preclude them from believing in God. At the same time, they need to understand that science does in fact need a cautionary word spoken by people of faith who believe ethics must guide science unless we do in fact eventually turn the mythical Frankenstein into reality.

The bond Christian skeptics share with science is a commitment to the pursuit of truth. In science theories are the best conclusions science can reach at any given moment. Honest theology has the same commitment. The goal for people of faith is not to get beyond doubt, but to see it as essential to understanding the world we believe has its origins in God. When you are not afraid of truth, you are not afraid of doubt, of skepticism, of a commitment to following evidence where it leads. That is how the pursuit of truth works. Jesus himself said that truth is the source of joy and freedom, not fear. "'If you continue or abide in my word, you are truly my disciples," he once said, "and you will know the truth, and the truth will make you free." (John 8:32-33) Continue or stay with ("meno") what I am telling you, Jesus says, and you will know "truth" (aletheia) that will make you free (léfteros).

Biblical interpreters have a variety of views about what this text means, but it comes down to perceiving the truth in Jesus' words that makes sense to us, and I suppose we could extend it to include the truth his actions also revealed. The truth Jesus talked about doesn't focus on what you believe, but what kind of person you are, how you think, speak, and act toward others. He said it directly when he highlighted the two great commandments. Loving God, i.e., devotion to God first, and loving your neighbor as you love yourself, i.e., treating others the way you want to be treated, (Matthew 22:36-40), these are what count.

The pursuit of truth is actually the common denominator between science and religion. Skepticism serves both in seeking answers to different questions. Science wades through questions born of doubt to find out what happened. Religion wades through questions born of doubt to find out why. As many scientists and people have found out, both pursuits can be in service to God.

†

5

READING THE BIBLE HONESTLY

"I believe in the Bible," was what the man said to me when he was challenging why the seminary where I taught had women students. I knew what he meant because I had heard it numerous times, but I was confident he didn't understand that what he was saying made no sense in light of how we got the Bible and what it actually is. For him, and many Christians like him, the Bible is their sole source of authority for what they believe all Christians must believe. Aside from the subjective nature of beliefs they either don't understand or refuse to believe, they are likely to be unaware of how the Bible came to be in the first place, a story anyone who appeals to the authority of the Bible should know if they want to read the Bible honestly.

Let's begin with the fact that the Jesus movement that became the church and in turn became Christianity both existed before the Bible was "the Bible." The process of what is called "canonization" or the formal establishment of the Christian Canon, i.e. authoritative writings, was both an oral and written process that took place over hundreds of years. Contrary to what some people think, the selection of which books to include and exclude was not the result of a church council making the decision independent of the people. It was, instead, something quite different, as Jerry Sumney, New Testament scholar and a former seminary colleague of mine, describes, "The faith community discussed and debated which writings should be authoritative until they reached a broad consensus."[27] He goes on to say,

In the end, the believing communities (postexilic and pre-rabbinic Jews for the Hebrew Bible and the early church for the New Testament) gathered these writings, claiming them as the texts by which they would lead their lives and derive their understanding of God, the world, and one another. They bequeathed those who followed them (the Jewish community and the church) as books that give life and engender relationship with God, as books in which later believers could also hear the voice of God.[28]

This history reminds us that both how the Bible was written and how it came to be called the church's sacred text was a process that could be described as purely organic. That is, it arose naturally as the original apostles (formerly disciples who had been with Jesus) passed away, creating the need for a new authority to guide the community. Books written by or attributed to one of the original apostles also gained immediate acceptance among the various faith communities throughout the Roman Empire. Church councils later selected the books to make up the Christian Bible that in large part had already been in use. The Bible we have today are those books early Christians found helpful and meaningful for their own lives. For background to what the church called the New Testament, church leaders also added the Torah (first five books) that had been formed by rabbis during the Babylonian captivity between 586–537 B.C.E. and the Writings, Prophets, and Wisdom Literature that constitute the Hebrew Bible or Jewish "canon." Because of the nature of the canonical process, it is more accurate to think of scriptural authority as initially from the bottom up rather than the top down. In other words, the books that gained authority did so because the people had already affirmed that authority through regular use of them.

The purpose of this process was to establish a standard by which the authority of all texts would be judged by the church. That is what the word "canon" means, "standard." The New Testament was not formerly canonized until 393 C.E. at the Council of Hippo and in 398 at the Council of Carthage, both in North Africa. The first full Bible was a Latin translation by St.

Jerome in the early 5th century known as The Latin Vulgate. Prior to the Latin Vulgate was the Septuagint which was a translation of the Hebrew Bible into Greek. The first Bible produced in Europe by a printing press was the Gutenberg Bible printed in 1454. Because it was printed on paper and various types of parchment, there were different versions of the same Gutenberg Bible. The Great Bible was the first authorized version approved by King Henry VIII in 1539.

Today, of course, there are thousands of versions of the Bible in multiple languages, but important to reading the Bible honestly is the fact that no manuscripts of the original Hebrew and Greek texts remain. All have been lost. Translators must use copies of copies, none of which is complete and many of which have missing parts for which translators must provide a text they think is most accurate. Some translations are simply translations of translations. There are also popular paraphrase versions of the Bible such as the Living Bible and The Message. The three branches of Christianity—Roman Catholic, Eastern Orthodox, and Protestant—have authorized different Bibles for use in their traditions. The Catholic Bible includes the 39 books of the Hebrew Bible, the 27 Christian scriptures, and the 14 books of the Apocrypha (books worthy of study, but to which no authority is ascribed). The Eastern Bible adds three other books to the Catholic Bible that are called "Deuterocanonical" books, which means of questionable origin and without authority. The Protestant Bible regardless of the translation consists of the 39 books of the Hebrew Bible and the 27 books of Christian scripture.

The Catholic Church avoided controversy about the authority of the Bible by establishing itself as the primary authority for Catholic teaching, or what is called church tradition. The Bible informs church teaching, but once the Catholic Church speaks, Catholics are supposed to listen. Catholic hierarchy doesn't claim acceptance of its authority is necessary to be Christian, only to be Catholic. Once the Protestant movement rejected the authority of the papacy, thus, the authority of the Roman Church itself, it elevated the Bible to that status, what some call Protestantism's paper pope." The two primary reformers, Martin Luther and John Calvin, both believed there had to be a substitute for church authority as a guide to faith and practice. Thus, the Bible quickly became "sola scriptura" for the nascent Protestant movement, meaning the sole source of authority for beliefs and practices.

Yet, Luther himself challenged the appropriateness of some books being in the Protestant Bible such as Hebrews, James, Jude, and Revelation. He also believed the Holy Spirit gave ordinary Christians interpretive guidance in understanding the Bible's message. "The Holy Scriptures," he wrote, "require a humble reader who shows reverence and fear toward the Word of God, and constantly says, 'teach me, teach me, teach me'… the Spirit resists the proud."[29] Luther advocated for the Bible to be translated into the vernacular of the people so they could encounter and experience the work of the Spirit that would make the "preaching of God" known to them.[30]

Calvin, whose leadership was centered in Geneva, Switzerland, was more insistent than Luther in a literal approach to interpreting scripture, completely rejecting the validity of seeing scripture through the lens of spiritual teaching and allegory. "But since we are not favored with daily oracles from heaven," he wrote, "and since it is only in the Scriptures that the Lord hath been pleased to preserve his truth in perpetual remembrance, it obtains the same complete credit and authority with believers, when they are satisfied of its divine origin, as if they heard the very words pronounced by God himself."[31]

The modern forms of biblical literalism[32] that insist either the words or theological content of the Bible were inspired by God and, thus, without mistake or error, are rooted in Calvin's view of scripture. Unlike Calvin, though, modern literalists use 2 Timothy 3:16-17 that speaks of the inspiration of scripture in justifying its view of scripture, but they are misreading what the text actually says. "All scripture is inspired by God, and is useful for teaching," it reads, "for reproof, for correction, and for training in righteousness, so that the person of God may be proficient, equipped for every good work." The Greek word for "inspired" (theopneustos) means "breathed out or breathed upon." It is similar to the Hebrew word "breath" or "spirit" (ruach) implied in Genesis 2:7: "God formed man from the dust of the ground and breathes into his nostrils the breath of life, and the man became a living being." Thus, when the 2 Timothy text says "all scripture is inspired," the likely meaning is that all scripture has been breathed out or been breathed upon by God and given life, and that the same breath of life is conveyed to readers as their minds and hearts connect with the words of the scripture.

Just as important to know is the fact that the word "scripture" in the text is referring to the Hebrew Bible since the New Testament did not exist at the time. In addition, inspiration is not an end in itself. It has a purpose, which is to teach and educate people in the ways of God and their response of doing good works. The text says nothing about the Bible being infallible or inerrant. To use these verses as a basis for such a claim is precisely what happens when you don't read the Bible honestly, and undermines the claim of biblical authority that accounts for literalism even being a thing. As the canonical process we've been discussing shows, this is not how biblical authority works. The authority of the books that made it into the Bible lies with the inward receptivity to them that pre-existed the establishment of the Canon.

The late United Methodist theologian, Albert Outler, also reminded us that biblical authority is only one of four sources of authority for Christians first articulated by John Wesley himself. Outler called it the Wesleyan Quadrilateral[33] that consisted of: (1) the Bible; (2) church tradition; (3) reason; (4) experience. Wesley himself believed all knowledge for Christians needed to be examined from these four perspectives, but insisted that biblical authority was pre-emminent to the other three. Personally, I have found it more helpful to consider all four as co-equals in regard to authority. It is a practical way to resist one exercising tyranny over the others in precisely the way biblical literalism does. Using your personal experiences, the teachings of the church, and your power of reasoning, the Bible can be a resource for and guide to being Christian in a world that is often resistant to truth.

The underlying point of the Wesleyan Quadrilateral, though, is the reality that any effort to impose biblical authority on others without regard for their own experiences, traditions, and capacity to think for themselves will meet with resistance, if not outright rejection. Maturity of faith is nurtured by reading the Bible honestly, drawing upon everything that influences and shapes our lives. To argue, for example, that Christians today must accept the views of the Apostle Paul regarding the role of women is to fight with windmills. In fact, it is understanding that Paul was reflecting an attitude consistent with the way women were seen by first century Judaism rather than the will of God allowing readers to weigh his words against their own views without being accused of not believing in the Bible. I think one of the missing elements in debates about the Bible today is its simple and beautiful humanness that connects modern Christians with ancient writers by making their theological perspective a basis for honest engagement rather than a matter of acceptance or rejection.

Ultimately, though, efforts to protect the Bible's authority end up ignoring or denying the logical fallacies we previously discussed about how the brain works. In this way literalism is an example of the strain of anti-intellectualism in American Christianity that has existed since the westward movement, as carefully documented in the 1963 Pulitzer Prize winning book by Richard Hofstadter entitled, Anti-intellectualism in American Life.[34] At bottom, biblical literalism is a sham that promotes the notion that God is afraid of the human ability to think. It's the equivalent of trying to convince adults that believing in Santa Claus is the only way to celebrate Christmas.

Equally important is the fact that biblical literalism is completely unnecessary. The Bible never has and doesn't now need to be defended. It needs to be understood. Scholarship provides information about how to read the Bible that helps readers better understand it. The multiple critical approaches scholars use in studying the Bible offer incredible insights into what the Bible says in ways that enrich its meaning instead of diminishing it. Lay Christians often forget that scholars are women and men of faith just as they are. Their goal is to make the biblical message understandable, not to undermine its authority. They know the Bible has stood the test of time without losing its place as the sacred text for Christians. Reading it honestly honors that place by uncovering the best understanding possible.

An example of how biblical scholarship facilitates reading the Bible honestly is by putting biblical texts in their historical context. When it comes to communications, context is indispensable to comprehending the writer's message. Consider song lyrics. The words of a song in and of themselves may touch you, but putting them in context can deepen their meaning . A good example is the hit song of the 60s entitled "Up On The Roof," made popular by the singing group The Drifters.

The melody was written by the iconic Carole King, the lyrics by her then husband, Gerry Goffin. On the face of it, the words seem ordinary with the tune carrying the song. But the context behind the lyrics changes that perspective. Goffin's father was a man of moods and was difficult to be around. As a teenager Goffin didn't know how to deal with his dad when he was in one of his moods so he would climb a staircase up to the roof of the apartment building to escape. Reflecting on his childhood years later he wrote these words:

> When this old world starts getting me down
> And people are just too much for me to face
> I climb way up to the top of the stairs
> And all my cares just drift right into space
>
> On the roof, it's peaceful as can be.
> And there the world below can't bother me
> Let me tell you now
>
> On the roof, the only place I know
> Where you just have to wish to make it so
> Let's go up on the roof.
> Up on the roof

Put in context, "Up On The Roof" takes on an entirely different meaning than it does if you hear the song without knowing that the words were born of the experience of a boy escaping the volatile moods of his father.[35] Context is, indeed, everything when you are communicating. That is also true when it comes to understanding the Bible. The gift of biblical scholars is that they explain the context of scriptural passages which helps readers grasp a fuller meaning of a text.

Of course, the many types of critical analysis of the Bible don't exhaust the full richness of reading the Bible honestly. Devotional reading offers its own spiritual enrichment. It sets scholarship aside and invites you to let biblical stories and verses speak to you because of who you are and the circumstances in your own life. Devotional reading doesn't focus on what the writer of a book intended to say. Rather, its concern is what a story or text says that helps you live the life you are capable of living. The Book of Job, for example, may help you reject the image of God as one who punishes or sends pain and suffering to test you. Or the simple text, "God is love" (1 John 4:8) may become the dominant image of God for your life. The point of devotional reading is for the Bible to be a resource for a view of life that gives it meaning and purpose. You can embrace some verses while ignoring others. The goal is to allow the Bible to inspire you to trust in the goodness of God, the goodness of life, the joy of relationships, the sacredness of creation, the power of love, and so forth.

Both scholarly study and devotional reading constitute an honest approach to the Bible that affirms your freedom to think for yourself as you seek to understand the biblical message for your own life. Anyone who tells you to accept the Bible as it is written is expressing a belief of their own to which you owe no allegiance. The Bible itself is a testimony of faith that invites you to ponder its witness in order to benefit from past wisdom and insight, but in no way are you obligated to embrace what it says as if truth is limited to its time and place in history. New insights add to the biblical witness rather than undermining it. The Bible is the church's book, but Christianity is larger than the Bible just as it is larger than the church.

Given what we know about how we got the Bible in the first place, and the human imprint on the biblical books themselves, I suggest the 19th century American journalist, William Lloyd Garrison, summarized the kind of attitude toward the Bible a Christian skeptic takes that sets the standard for how to read the Bible honestly:

To say that everything contained within the lids of the Bible is divinely inspired, and to insist upon the dogma as fundamentally important, is to give utterance to a bold fiction, and to require the suspension of the reasoning faculties. To say that everything in the Bible is to be believed, simply because it is found in that volume, is equally absurd and pernicious. To discard a portion of scripture is not necessarily to reject the truth, but may be the highest evidence that one can give of his love of truth.[36]

Garrison captured the true purpose of Christian skepticism, especially in its pursuit of truth about God, Jesus, the spirit of God within us, the environment that surrounds us, and points the direction for how to be Christian in a society that is intentionally and constitutionally secular for its own good and that of religion as well.

6

REMEMBERING WHO'S ON FIRST

As it turns out, this chapter has proven to be the most difficult to write, which upon reflection is as it should be. To speak of God is serious business. Judaism does not speak the name of God directly in deference to the holiness of God. While I do use the name God, I do with a sense of awe for the One I believe is appropriately called the Creator and Sustainer of life. It in fact troubles me when I hear Christians speak of God in careless and thoughtless ways, as if they know who God is and believe that God must in fact be who they say God is. It seems to me that a fundamental presumption when writing or speaking of God is to admit that whatever one believes about God cannot and does not fully encompass the totality of who God is. In short, God is always more than what we believe about God.

The place I think to begin in talking about God is where both the Hebrew and Christian Bibles begin: "In the beginning God" says Genesis 1:1. It all starts with God. Not with the Bible. Not with Judaism. Not with Christianity. The beginning and ending, the alpha and omega, is God. Not anything else. Not anyone else. Not even Jesus. Without God Jesus has no purpose, but without Jesus God remains God. God is always the fundamental issue for people of faith. If God is real, the way you live changes. If God is not real, religious beliefs become little more than superstition. The challenge to Christians is not to make Jesus divine, as we will discuss in the next chapter. It is to make God believable.

To talk about God is inevitably to talk about the mystery that lies at the heart of everything that is. Mystery is not the same thing as something that is hard to understand or comprehend. It means, rather, trusting that something is real even if unknown, based on human experience. Love is mystery and at the same time real, which is why your heart leaps when your beloved walks in the room. Mystery is feeling your own heart break when someone else's already has. It is the amazing joy you feel in seeing racial blindness in children who pay no attention to skin color when choosing friends. Mystery is present in daily life in ways we take for granted, but are nonetheless real.

Scientists say they know about 10% of what the universe is and what is in it. The rest is mystery, waiting to be known while knowing it will never be fully known. That is how I think about God, a reality that cannot be seen, heard, or touched, but can be known. Not in the ways facts are known. Not the kind of knowing scientists affirm, but a knowing that points to an inner truth that not everything that is real can be explained. Brother David Steindl-Rast describes it as truth that holds on to us more than we hold on to it. "We know that religion has something to do with truth," he writes, "but it isn't the truth that we can grab and grasp and take home with us...the real truth that we are after is something that holds us; it holds us when we give ourselves, in those moments when we really open ourselves." He adds, "That's what life is and that's what religious life is...giving ourselves to the truth, not taking the truth, grasping the truth, holding the truth. It's only the truth to which we give ourselves that will make us free."[37]

This kind of knowing exists for those who are willing to embrace ultimate mystery. It's called faith, not an irrational response to randomness or the need for meaning and purpose, simply a humble acknowledgement that what is known in the traditional sense of scientific knowing is not all the reality there is. That is how I believe in God as a Christian skeptic. I am not a theistic skeptic. I am not withholding judgment about the reality of God until I find more evidence one way or the other. That is a search with no end. Believing in God is an affirmation of a kind of knowing with eyes wide open to mystery.

But mere believing in God is only part of the choice a person of faith makes. What matters more is the image of God you have once you choose to believe in God. Both the Hebrew and Christian Bibles portray various and often conflicting images of God. Any image of God is about the attributes you believe best describe God.[38] There are two primary attributes of God that form the image I have. The first is personal. I don't mean that I believe God is a person, rather, that God is personal, one who knows me, knows humanity, and wants the best for us. This is how Israel's God was distinct from the cultural gods of Canaan and the pantheon of Greek and Roman gods. God heard the people's cry and came down to rescue them, as Exodus 3:7-8 declares, "I have observed the misery of my people who are in Egypt; I have heard their cry on account of their taskmasters. Indeed, I know their sufferings, and I have come down to deliver them from the Egyptians and to bring them up out of that land to a good and spacious land, to a land flowing with milk and honey."

I understand the warning about Christian anthropomorphism, the practice of assigning human characteristics to God, but in the Hebrew Bible the writers speak of God using human qualities, not to suggest God is human, but to underscore the personal nature of God who knows the creation and sees the suffering of the people, hears their cry of help, and chooses to respond to their needs. The Torah speaks of the God of the Mosaic covenant as one who is relatable, personable, knowable. The Christian belief in Jesus as the incarnation of God, God in the flesh, was, I believe, intended to convey this same image of God. The incarnation of Jesus was a way to convey the message that God is personable, relatable, one who knows and can be known, one who shows compassion, forgives, does not forsake covenant.

The most positive image of God in scripture is loving. The Gospel of John describes Jesus as the gift of love God has given to the world in need of redemption: "For God so loved the world that he gave his only Son, so that everyone who believes in him may not perish but may have eternal life." (3:16) In the next two chapters we will discuss who Jesus was and the Christian concept of salvation. Here the point is that a primary image of God in both Hebrew and Christian scripture is that God is personal and God is loving. The First Letter of John summed it up this way: "God is love, and those who abide in love abide in God, and God abides in them." (4:16) In this context, the writer is not saying God is love in the sense that love defines who God is. Rather, he is saying that God is loving, and the way to experience God is giving and receiving love.

We find this theme in numerous places in Hebrew scripture. The prophet Jeremiah wrote, "I have loved you with an everlasting love; therefore I have continued my faithfulness to you." (31:3) Zephaniah declared, "The Lord, your God, is in your midst, a warrior who gives victory; he will rejoice over you with gladness; he will renew you in his love; he will exult over you with loud singing. (3:17) Psalm 136 repeats again and again: "O give thanks to the Lord, for he is good, for his steadfast love endures forever." Lamentations 3:22-23 says, "The steadfast love of the Lord never ceases; his mercies never come to an end; they are new every morning; great is your faithfulness." Isaiah 43:25 declares, "I, I am he who blots out your transgressions for my own sake, and I will not remember your sins."

Jesus, of course, lived and taught the same message, only he added two aspects of God being loving that are extremely provocative. The first is that God loves unconditionally. This is most clearly seen in the Parable of the Prodigal Son (Luke 15:11-32), but is often missed entirely by focusing on verse 17 that says, "But when he came to his senses." That phrase may not mean what you think it means. The traditional interpretation is that this rebellious son finally sees the foolishness of his ways and goes home to his family and is welcomed with open arms by his father and that is how God welcomes sinners who repent. But the rest of the verse suggests that is not what the story is actually saying.

When the son comes to his senses, his first thought is not that he realizes how foolish he has been. Instead, he realizes where he can get something to eat: "How many of my father's hired hands have bread enough and to spare, but here I am dying of hunger!" is what he first thinks about. He knows what he needs to do. He needs to go home, but he has to make his father believe he has seen the light so he makes a plan: "I will get up and go to my father, and I will say to him, 'Father, I have sinned against heaven and before you; I am no longer worthy to be called your son; treat me like one of your hired hands'." (17b-19)

He is, of course, counting on his father doing no such thing, that being the loving man he is means he will welcome him back into the family as the son he is. And that is what makes the older brother angry. He knows his younger brother well, that he's a conniver, that he's coming home only because he's broke and half starving. The older brother tries to convince his father not to trust the prodigal, but the father insists both of his sons are and always will be sons.

The key question the parable asks us is, "What did the prodigal do the next day?" Was the father right about him or was the older brother? When the prodigal came to his senses, did that mean what we hope it meant, or did it mean he was no fool, that he knew he could go home, re-group, and take off again when he got the chance. The fact is, we don't know the answer, and neither did the father and that is the point of the parable. He welcomed him home with open arms, not because the prodigal had changed, but because the father's love was unconditional.

That is what I think Jesus was saying about God. Divine love is always welcoming. It has no conditions. It depends on who God is and not on what we do or don't do. It sounds foolish, of course, as foolish as a shepherd leaving ninety-nine sheep vulnerable to the dangers of being in the wilderness without protection to go search for one sheep that has strayed. (Matthew 18:10-14) But Jesus did more than talk about God's love being unconditional. He lived the same way. He welcomed a tax-collector who was a Jew working for the Roman government into his circle of closest friends (Luke 5:27-28), embraced a woman supposedly caught in the act of adultery (John 8:1-11), and told his disciples that a Samaritan man they had been taught to hate could show more compassion than the highest-ranking Jewish official. (Luke 10:25-37)

This is the God I believe in, a God who is loving, a God whose love is radical to the point of going beyond what seems reasonable and takes the chance that its power lies precisely in just how radical it is. But, of course, the people of God have always had trouble trusting in unconditional love. We believe in God, but our image of God is more of a judge who hands out sentences than one who is merciful, not surprisingly, given that the most prominent book in the Torah is Deuteronomy whose theme is the ethic of blessings and curses. On the one hand it affirms the goodness of God who blesses the nation when the people are faithful to the covenantal laws of Moses, but places equal emphasis on the punishment of the nation if the people abandoned God. It fits into the image of Israel's God, Yahweh, as the only true God above all others, which meant Yahweh was in control of everything. Nothing happened outside the purview of Yahweh. This in turn led to what we call "radical monotheizing" in which the biblical writers declare that God is in control of everything that happens, including battles Israel won and lost. Victory and defeat equally depended on Israel's obedience to God. Not only was victory a sign of blessing, but defeat was a sign of divine curse.

So dominant was the Deuteronomic ethic that it eventually became inverted and used as an indicator of who was good and who was bad. When something good happened it meant God was blessing the people (or person) for their obedience. When something bad happened, it meant God was punishing them for their disobedience. The three friends in the story of Job represent this inversion of the Deuteronomic ethic, friends Job describes as "miserable comforters are you all (16:2), rejecting their faith in the ethic of blessings and curses. We know, of course, that Job is right and they are wrong because of his being "a man blameless and upright" (v.1:1), which is the basis for the wager between God and the Satan who says Job will fold when he faces hardship. Jesus also rejected the ethic when he made the simple statement that the rain falls upon the just and the unjust alike. ((Matthew 5:45)

Yet, the Deuteronomic ethic shows up in the thinking of Christians today in the most unexpected ways. Recently a woman college basketball star said in an interview after she had led her team to a critical victory that she could not have done what she did without God's help. The year before she had suffered a serious injury that prevented her from playing that season. Coming back and achieving the quality of play she had demonstrated before her injury was an amazing accomplishment. She interpreted her ordeal as God testing her faith, stretching her to limits she didn't know she could go, but she had remained faithful and God had rewarded her with a renewal of her basketball career, in her mind proving God is always in control.

She didn't know it, of course, but this was not only a modern version of the Deuteronomic ethic, it was an example of radical monotheizing. She had a serious injury she interpreted as God's way of testing her faithfulness. The same can be said of sentiments frequently expressed in phrases such as "God doesn't put anything on us God doesn't think we can handle" or more pointed, "Everything that happens is the will of God." Sadly, this is what people have learned and are still hearing from the church. For some reason Christians find it easier to attribute everything to God even if it presents an image of God as the source of evil as well as good. They may find comfort in believing in this kind of God, but that has not been my experience. I keep thinking of members of the team that lost to the victorious team led by the young basketball star mentioned earlier who were in tears at the end of the game. Was that God's doing? Or the parents of the child who dies in the same hospital where parents of another child who lives says it was all because of God?

The belief that God is ultimately in control of everything has two primary problems that go beyond the awful image of God it portrays. One is that it creates a quid pro quo relationship between God and humankind. You give me something and I will give you something. You do me a favor in exchange for me doing you one. In like manner, God blesses us in return for our being obedient, but we suffer the consequences if we aren't. It's the way the deal works. We try to be good, God will give us something good in return.

The second problem with believing God is in control is worse than the first one. It undermines belief in free will. If, as new England preacher Jonathon Edwards said, it is only by the hand of God holding us over a pit of fire that keeps us from being consumed for eternity in it, how can free will mean anything? Edwards did acknowledge that "there was no Want of Power in God to cast wicked men into Hell at any moment."[39] But there is nothing to prevent God from doing so save the decision of the wicked to enter into the covenant of grace in Christ. Edwards may have been the extreme voice for an image of God as a coercive judge and executioner before whom every sinner will stand, but he was by no means the only one. The threat of hell has been a singular theme in traditional theology without any effort to explain how free will is free when that threat supersedes the choice to live for or against God's will. That is why I contend that the image of God as one who controls everything and the concept of free will are irreconcilable opposites.

The only image of God that takes free will seriously is God extending unconditional love to all humanity. It fits perfectly with the belief that God is love. Think about it this way. Loving parents do not want to control everything in their children's lives, including the decisions they make, in order to protect them or to ensure they always do what their parents want them to do. Parents, of course, are smart enough to know they have no such control, but loving parents don't want that kind of control because it would make their child's decisions and behavior the parents' instead of the child's. Choosing to do what is right would have no meaning for the child. Personal morality would be rendered meaningless because moral choice would be eliminated.

The same has to be true in the divine/human relationship. If God is in complete control, obedience to the will of God means nothing. It means everything, though, if God's love for the humanity to which God gave breath is inexhaustible, unconditional, and is forever. Only then does dedicating your life to live in a way that pleases God mean anything. The image of a God who loves unconditionally naturally co-exists with a belief in free will. They in fact give meaning to one another. I believe a God who loves us enough to grant us the freedom to make decisions about how we live is a God who does not coerce devotion, which is the only way loving God in return has meaning and substance. Coerced love, ever how subtle, is fake or inauthentic love.

To summarize where we are. The most compelling image I find in scripture is God is love, unconditional love. I choose to believe in a loving God because I am willing to embrace mystery as part of life. I confess that sometimes the image of God behind the way some people speak of God causes me to wonder why they believe in God at all. The comfort they apparently find in the notion that God is always in control of everything that happens is an enigma to me. I am unable to see what purpose life could have if we are little more than marionettes who appear to have free movement, but in fact have none because free will is ultimately controlled by a God who punishes if we don't obey.

But Jesus goes further. He says the way we are to express gratitude for God's unconditional love is by loving other people. While the two great commandments he talked about—loving God with all your mind, heart, soul, and strength, and loving your neighbor as you love yourself—were already in the Torah (Deuteronomy 6:5; Leviticus 19:18), Jesus put them together and defined loving your neighbor as the way to show love for God. (Matthew 22:36-40) But he didn't stop there. He said that loving your neighbor, as good as that is, didn't go far enough. It had to be extended to people you consider your enemies (echthros), someone who is openly hostile to you or someone who shows enmity toward you. (Matthew 5:44-45)

Loving others without conditions is a serious demand on how we live. Failing at it is not an excuse for not trying, and persistent trying is the way we choose to be in relationship with God. It is the way anyone who loves God lives, another way of saying that life begins with God who loves unconditionally and calls us to love the same way. The fact that Torah law and the teachings of Jesus call us to loving others highlights the connectedness we humans share with one another. As it turns out, we actually are made for one another. Living is about relationships. The Genesis story of Adam and Eve says that God knew it was not a good thing for man to be alone, thus, woman was created as a co-equal to man. (2:18) The Hebrew word in this text is helper (ezer) or "suitable helper" (ezer kenegdo), one who is more than a helper, but has the power to help, even to rescue. The word is also used in scripture to refer to God as Israel's helper.[40]

The message should be clear. We humans were created to be together. We are not to be alone, solely on our own. We are part of one another. Because God is creator, we, the creation, the creatures, belong to one another. David Steindl-Rast reminds us that religion is "literally the re-tying of ligaments that have been torn, bonds that connect us with all of creation, with our true self, and with the Divine."[41] It is a truth we experience daily. There is nothing that brings us more joy and at the same time opens us to emotional pain and even spiritual anguish more than the love we share with family, friends, neighbors, colleagues, and beyond. This is what Christianity is about—relationships.

It cannot be said enough that the image of God you have is critically important, and that image is a choice you have to make for yourself. The Bible has no single image of God, but whatever image of God you embrace will influence not only how you think of God, but how you treat other people. You are the one to make this choice, a free choice that has consequences not of God's making, but your own. There are consequences to what we say and do, no better expressed in the words of the Apostle Paul's words when he wrote, "Do not be deceived," he wrote, "God is not mocked, for you reap whatever you sow. If you sow to your own flesh, you will reap corruption from the flesh; but if you sow to the Spirit, you will reap eternal life from the Spirit. (Galatians 6:7) No one rescues us from the consequences of our own behavior, but in all cases those consequences are a result of our actions, not God's judgment.

The fundamental point scripture makes, and certainly the teachings of Jesus, is that we can trust ourselves to God's love. It is the heart of the relationship God has with us. Thus, living a life that pleases God is its own reward because it brings joy and peace like nothing else does, joy and peace not subject to circumstances that outwardly contradict both. But the image you have of God holds the key to your belief in God being the source of joy and peace it can be.

Making the choice to believe in a God whose love is unconditional has always been made easier for me because of my own parents. I was fortunate enough to have parents I knew loved me and my brothers unconditionally. I never had to question that, only to trust it. I was well aware of decisions I made that pleased and displeased them, caused them joy and caused them sorrow, but at no point did I ever have to worry that they would reject me. My brothers experienced them the same way. Not everyone is so fortunate to have such parents, but the fact that many parents are like the ones I had proves that we humans have the capacity to love unconditionally, and people of faith believe God is the reason why. We don't believe the best qualities we have are the by-product of nothingness. Rather, they are part of our nature because they are the very nature of God who made us.

God, then, is the cornerstone of faith. Saying that seems to be stating the obvious, yet in my experience Christians easily forget that in the beginning there was God and nothing else. The first decision Christians make in order to be Christian is, strangely, not to believe in Jesus. It is to believe in God. We don't believe in God because we believe in Jesus. We believe in Jesus because we believe in God. Remembering that is essential as we think about who Jesus was, which is the subject to which we now turn our attention.

7

ROOM IN THE INN FOR JESUS

I was taught to believe Jesus was the divine son of God. It was not until I realized there was no need for Jesus to be divine to be an instrument of God that everything about him changed for me. His being human was enough. The divine Jesus lost all meaning for me, even if he remains the cornerstone for traditional Christian beliefs, as summarized succinctly by British evangelical theologian David Wenham in this statement:

> It does matter enormously whether we regard the Bible's teaching in its entirety as God's Word and whether we see Jesus as a fallible or infallible teacher. It does matter enormously whether we believe you can come to God through other religions than that of Jesus, and whether we believe that people's eternal destiny is decided by their response to Jesus in this life, or whether there is a second chance beyond. It does matter whether we believe that practicing homosexuality is always wrong or sometimes right.[42]

Notice that the first defense of the divine Jesus, son of God, is to throw scripture at skeptics to prove they are wrong. But "proof texting" is a slippery slope that runs both ways. I will also offer scripture later in the chapter to support my perspective, making me vulnerable to being accused of "proof texting" as well, which is the point, actually. While I seek to cite texts in a way that is faithful to what reasonable interpretations suggest is their meaning, theological arguments are unavoidably subjective. I don't cite texts to prove a point, but to prove there are other ways of understanding biblical texts (and Jesus) than what traditional

Christianity says. Neither is provable or the "right" perspective, nor should either be considered a definitive statement about who Jesus was.

Of course, saying anything about Jesus presupposes that he actually lived. Whether he did or not is a matter of debate in some circles, but of no importance in our discussion. Personally, it stretches my imagination to the breaking point for there to have been more than fifty gospels written about a man who never lived without someone decisively exposing the fraud of their works. Thus, what I say about Jesus presupposes that he was an actual person, a man whose life became a catalyst for the formation of the world's dominant religious tradition.

That said, everything else we say about Jesus is what we believe about him, not necessarily who he was. Indeed, what we believe about Jesus is based on what the people who knew him in person believed about him. We have no first-hand knowledge of Jesus, only the testimonies of what those who did know him believed about him. In addition, we know the historical context in which he lived. Everything else we know is through faith and that is a different kind of knowing, an inward truth for our lives that transcends factual knowledge. That means you cannot prove what you believe about Jesus is true, nor can anyone prove it isn't. The content of faith is subjective and personal. It is harmful only if it leads you to believe things about yourself that are unhealthy or leads you to speak or act in harmful ways toward others.

If you have trouble believing that Jesus was both human and divine, and/or believing it makes you less likely to consider yourself Christian, what follows will help you. As I have already said, Jesus doesn't need to be divine for him to be the reason Christianity exists or for his life to have relevance for your life. For one thing, when Jesus was born non-Jews in the Roman Empire already believed that men could be gods. Caesar was believed to be a god. The sons of Caesar were called the sons of god. It was this social context from which the belief that Jesus was divine arose.

Further, that belief spread among non-Jewish Christians once the church became predominantly Gentile as the Jesus movement became distinct from Judaism. Had it remained a sect within Judaism, the story of Jesus would hav⟨ quite different. Instead, the Jesus removed from ⟩ faith became a divine figure that took on a life o⟨ suggest became a distraction from who he actually w⟨ you believe Jesus died for the sins of the world, God cou⟨ accomplished that without his being divine. Moreover, the tru⟨ of his teachings stands on the power of the wisdom in them. He didn't need to be infallible to speak truth, as has been the case with people before and since him. The authority of his words lay in the truth he spoke that connected with the truth that already existed within his followers.

It was when I began to take Jesus' humanity seriously that his life and teachings took on existential significance rather than remaining the object of my beliefs. It began when I read a book entitled, The Transforming Friendship.[43] It was my experience of meeting Jesus again for the first time others had when they read the book with that title by the late scholar, Marcus Borg.[44] Written many years ago by British clergyman, Leslie Weatherhead, Senior Minister at the famed British Temple, London, The Transforming Friendship was similar to what Borg wrote about but more provocative because it was written at a time when belief in Jesus as the divine son of God was taken for granted. Weatherhead, who described his religion as "nonconformist Christianity,"[45] dared to paint a different picture of the Jesus from the church's, one in which Jesus was fully and completely human, a way of seeing Jesus at a time when I found the Jesus of the church too divine to matter in the world I was living in where Christians were still insisting racial segregation was the will of God. A divine Jesus made no sense to me. The Jesus Weatherhead wrote about did, someone with whom I made an immediate connection because he was so human. Weatherhead connected humanity with divinity in a way that in this life made them essentially one:

> There is a sense in which every [person] is an incarnation of God. Divinity is not in a different category of thought from humanity. Divinity does not consist in an ability to do wonderful things like make stars or healing paralytics. These achievements may require power, but not necessarily

divinity. The meaning of divinity will be understood when we can get away from those values to moral values, not power to heal a paralytic but pure desire to do so; for divinity shines in love, compassion, lowliness of heart, passion to serve and uplift, to comfort and strengthen; and, to the extent to which a [person] is good—in the best sense, the most virile sense of that great word—to that extent [a person] manifests in his/her humanity the very nature of God...Let us try to learn the lesson then, God, whom so many of us think far off, is near to us, near us in our fellows.[46]

This Jesus made sense to me, and so did the God he served. "He revealed," wrote Weatherhead, "in that brief life and death the eternal nature of the loving heart of God."[47] It was not so much that what the church said about Jesus turned me away from God. It was, instead, that I couldn't see God in myself by looking at Jesus because he was already God and not human like me. Weatherhead gave me a new understanding of divinity and humanity as he described Jesus as being divine because he was so perfectly human: "Divinity stands most clearly revealed and most perfectly understood in perfect humanity."[48]

There it was, I thought. Humanity and divinity as one, not as God, but as God's creation, a man so wholly human that he was intimately connected to God as a vine is connected to a branch and who was inviting me to experience a similar connection. (John 15:1-9) Jesus was divine as a child of God in the same way that I am, you are, we all are. Years later Borg's book, though he interpreted Jesus in a different way than Weatherhead had, nonetheless connected with millions of Christians who found meaning in Jesus the man. What else did they need? If they wanted to commit themselves to the teachings of Jesus and live as best they could the way he lived, thereby, reminding the world of who he was, what could beliefs about his divinity add?

The question, of course, is, "Why am I still Christian? Why not a Jew? Why not a Muslim? Why not something else?" My answer is that I believe in God, but I am not a Jew because I don't follow Torah law, observe Torah rituals, and don't celebrate Torah holy days. I believe in God, but I am not a Muslim because

I don't follow the teachings of Islam. I believe in God, but I am Christian because I was raised Christian and continue to be inspired by the life Jesus lived and find truth and wisdom in his teachings. I know church teaching about Jesus as Christ, Messiah, God incarnate, savior of the world, the means of redemption for a fallen humanity, all of which I have studied my entire adult life and none of which has ever helped me understand who Jesus was beyond being a first century rabbi who had a small group of followers who travelled with him as he went from place to place teaching anyone who would listen about the ways of God.

Even those who were in that group struggled to answer the key question Jesus had asked them early on, "But who do you say that I am?" (Matthew 16:15) After the resurrection they made it clear they still had no answer: "Lord, is this the time when you will restore the kingdom to Israel?" (Acts 1:6) The truth about Jesus is that he was not easily understood then and still remains so today. It doesn't help that what little we know about him is limited primarily to the four gospels that describe who he was in very different ways. Matthew's Jesus is the new Moses who gives new commandments. Mark's Jesus is "the son of man," a title that comes from the Book of Daniel, but has no definitive meaning because Daniel is an apocalyptic story written during the Babylonian captivity that began in 586 B.C.E. and essentially makes who Jesus is mystery. Luke's Jesus is a messiah who upsets traditional Jews with his talk about Gentiles being included in God's covenant with Jews. John's Jesus comes down from heaven as a divine figure who dies on the cross, is raised to new life, and returns to God in heaven after giving the power of the Holy Spirit to the disciples.

Theological diversity wherein the nature of Jesus was seriously contested began immediately after his crucifixion and resurrection. It was not until the Nicene Creed of 325 C.E. that the church began to force conformity of belief in Jesus as the divine son of God. The doctrine of the Trinity was the result, declaring that the one true God had three manifestations—Father, Son, Holy Spirit. The church even found the doctrine in the words of Jesus himself when he said, "All authority in heaven and on earth has been given to me. Go therefore and make disciples of all nations, baptizing them in the name of the Father and of the Son and of the Holy Spirit." (Matthew 28:18-19) The problem was—and is—that if Jesus actually said these words, and scholars question whether the claim is true, it would have been unthinkable that as a Jew he would have claimed he shared equal divinity with God or that God existed in three persons.

Besides, nothing in Hebrew scripture suggests the people of Israel believed the messiah would be divine, equal to or of the same substance as God. Their radical monotheism made that a theological impossibility. Jesus as messiah and also divine mixes incompatible concepts. A divine messiah would have been an oxymoron to first century Jews, if not heretical. What is more, my own experience has been that it is completely unnecessary to being Christian. Seeing Jesus as a man and only a man has not diminished my own commitment to following the way he lived and taught. Jesus spoke and behaved in non-conventional ways, we might even say radical ways. He was provocative because he was an ordinary person himself with extraordinary charisma that attracted attention to what he was saying and doing. That's the Jesus who began to make sense to me even as what it might mean to follow him gave me pause. It was easy to prefer the divine Jesus who could easily be dismissed as a figure beyond my understanding or experience. Keeping a divine Jesus at armslength was easier than seeing him as a man like me who was devoted to the ethic of love and kindness and justice more than I was.

That is the irony of the struggle to know who Jesus was and is. The more divine the church makes him, the less seriously you have to take him. Trying to be like God becomes a dismissible absurdity. He sets an example you have no chance of following. But the more human Jesus is, the more he becomes an example you have to take seriously in how you live in a way that echoes the way he lived. Understand him as a man who may have been a mystic, a prophet, a rabbi makes more sense to Christian skeptics. For me the concept of friend made the critical difference. Friendship is not a common way to think of our relationship with Jesus. It may strike you as too familiar, even hokey, maudlin, or solipsistic, but the Apocryphal book, Ecclesiasticus ben Sirach, speaks of it in inspiring, poetic language:

> A faithful friend is a sturdy shelter:
> he that has found one has found a treasure.
> There is nothing so precious as a faithful friend,
> and no scales can measure his excellence.
> A faithful friend is an elixir of life;
> and those who fear the Lord will find him.
>   (Sirach 6:14-16)

Faithful friendship is a treasure in life, medicine for the soul, so to speak. The late French-born American writer Anaïs Nin described friendship this way, "Each friend represents a world in us, a world possibly not born until they arrive, and it is only by this meeting that a new world is born." Friendship, she adds, can create "joy, companionship, and growth—enriching our entire experience of the world."[49]

Isn't that what happens to us spiritually when we meet Jesus the man again for the first time that enables us to form a bond of friendship that transcends time and becomes a treasure in our lives, a relationship that impacts us to such an extent that it causes us to want to live differently, be different in the world than we otherwise would be? Instead of our being born again, a new world is born for us. The life we have known feels like it has been redeemed from mediocrity and meaninglessness with a sense of freedom and joy we did not know until the bond of friendship happened.

Jesus must have been comfortable thinking about his relationship to his disciples in this way. "I do not call you servants any longer," he told them, "because the servant does not know what the master is doing, but I have called you friends, because I have made known to you everything that I have heard from my Father." (John 15:15) They didn't fully understand what he was telling them, but enough that Jesus felt his relationship with them had changed from servant-master to friends. Diane Butler Bass describes it this way:

> Imagine how Jesus's close followers felt when they heard those words for the first time. Jesus brought them to the very heart of God and then revealed that God's heart longed

for friendship. They had heard this story before. They were more than servants to God. God was their friend; and they were friends of God. Servanthood, although admirable, is the lesser thing. Friendship, the knowing, loving, and free and joyful giving to another, is the passionate desire of God.[50]

And so it is with us when our thoughts move from his being divine to his being so thoroughly human that we connect with him in our very soul and join in the work he began of making the world better. I think Bass captured the reason why this is the experience when she also wrote, "Friendship is contingent on love—real love: compassion, empathy, reaching out, going beyond what we imagine is possible. That is the command: love. And if we reach out in love, friendship is the result, even friendship with God. Friendship is mutual, a hand extended and another reaching back."[51]

My wife, Joy, shared a prayer in a group of Christian skeptics who meet regularly and read this book in its early stages that also captured the efficacy of friendship in the way we have been discussing it:

O God, if anything makes us rich, it is our friends.
We could offer a litany of names of those we call friend.
In the truest sense of that word, people who let us be fully ourselves, with whom we feel relaxed, comfortable, at home.
In the mystery of your spirit, our souls find kinship.

We move through the risky places, hard questions,
even ordinary days, knowing our friends walk with us,
and taste the salt from our tears.
Our stories connect in strange and wonderful ways,
creating a coming history.

We bring our friends to you, O God, in this prayer;
younger friends who call us to life and wonder,
who open the places in our souls we closed long ago;
older friends who mentor for us the vision of experience

and see treasures in us we do not see in ourselves;
friends of our own generation who share common memories.
God, hear our prayer for our friends.
For our friends who are risking what is safe and familiar,
we offer the security of our care.
For our friends facing times so difficult they wonder
if they will ever breathe easily again,
we offer our hearts beating as one with theirs.
For our friends who are separated from us by the distance
of geography or spirit,
we offer the vulnerability of our love.

O God, we see in Jesus
the ultimate model of friendship,
and ask for the grace to follow his example,
that by grace we may pass that gift on to others. Amen

Jesus, friend of all humanity, a man for all seasons, all occasions, for all people. It is his humanity that connects him to us and us to him. It is the reason being Christian makes sense, why we have reason to believe we can live our lives as authentically as he lived his.

†

8

REDUNDANT SALVATION

Heaven: A place baptized Catholics and repentant Protestants go after they die.

Hell: A place of punishment for unbaptized Catholics and unrepentant Protestants.

Purgatory: A place the Catholic Church teaches baptized, but impure souls go to atone for their remaining sins in order to enter into heaven, sometimes referred to as a "cleansing fire."

Limbo: A place where unbaptized babies go that is not heaven, but better than hell. Recently Catholic theologians have suggested there is still hope that babies in Limbo might be saved.

For Christian skeptics, these beliefs alone make it difficult to believe in the concept of personal salvation. Not only do they lack any modicum of intellectual substance, they fly in the face of the known universe where space is essentially endless. The notion that "places" exist in the universe as the church describes them deserves the label "absurd." But it also illustrates the element of human limitation, including logical fallacies of the brain that influence everything the church says. Worst of all, believing in such "places" contradict believing in God. If God truly is, by definition God is infinite, not subject to time and space. If God occupies a place such as heaven, or created realms called "hell," "purgatory," or "limbo," that is a perfect argument against believing in the existence of God. God cannot exist in categories of time and space and be God.

The reason these beliefs arose in the first place is because of the concept of personal salvation that itself is a natural extension of the Deuteronomic ethic of blessings and curses we discussed in the chapter on God. The problem is that such beliefs have contributed to shifting attention away from how to live by the teachings of Jesus to a demand for right beliefs based on the emphasis the Apostle Paul placed on personal salvation. But there is a different way of understanding what Paul said that focuses on communal salvation rather than individual or personal, as in this text:

> So if anyone is in Christ, there is a new creation: everything old has passed away; look, new things have come into being! All this is from God, who reconciled us to himself through Christ and has given us the ministry of reconciliation; that is, in Christ God was reconciling the world to himself, not counting their trespasses against them, and entrusting the message of reconciliation to us. So we are ambassadors for Christ, since God is making his appeal through us; we entreat you on behalf of Christ: be reconciled to God. (2 Corinthians 5:17-20)

The key to understanding what Paul is saying is Judaism's concept of community. Jews have never believed in individual salvation apart from the community as a whole. When we examine the words of the text, the first thing to note is that "anyone" (tis) is a neutral pronoun used as a literary device. Anyone is everyone for whom God has now brought into the Mosaic covenant. Everyone is part of the creation God has fashioned anew. Individuals experience the new creation by being "in" Christ, but it is the creation that has been made new, not individuals. The "we" to whom Paul refers are Christians who like him are appealing to Jews and non-Jews to embrace their reconciled relationship with God before the end of the age Paul believed was imminent.

Eugene Peterson's "The Message" underscores this reading in his paraphrase of the text:

Because of this decision we don't evaluate people by what they have or how they look. We looked at the Messiah that way once and got it all wrong, as you know. We certainly don't look at him that way anymore. Now we look inside, and what we see is that anyone united with the Messiah gets a fresh start, is created new. The old life is gone; a new life emerges! Look at it! All this comes from the God who settled the relationship between us and him, and then called us to settle our relationships with each other. God put the world square with himself through the Messiah, giving the world a fresh start by offering forgiveness of sins. God has given us the task of telling everyone what he is doing. We're Christ's representatives. God uses us to persuade men and women to drop their differences and enter into God's work of making things right between them. We're speaking for Christ himself now: Become friends with God; he's already a friend with you.

What these words suggest is that Paul believed Jesus was the Messiah, but not in the political sense other Jews did wherein he would re-establish the kingdom of Israel. Instead, Paul believed Jesus was the Messiah, the anointed one, whose death was an act of God in which the sins of everyone, Jew and non-Jew alike, led God to create a new humanity, represented by the resurrection of Jesus. In this new creation not even death can end what God has done. This life is a taste of life eternal with God who is forever. In short, Jesus death was a sign that God has chosen to be reconciled with all humanity erasing all old categories, including divisions that separate. Paul expressed it this way: "There is neither Jew nor Greek, there is neither slave nor free, there is neither male nor female; for you are all one in Christ Jesus." (Galatians 3:28-29) Not only would salvation for a Jew without salvation for all Jews been inconceivable for Paul, salvation only for Jews was as well.

He came to this realization because of two experiences. The first was a growing Jewish resistance to believing Jesus was messiah and the second was non-Jews or Gentiles responding to Paul's message about God's new creation that included everyone.

In the context of this unexpected turn of events, Paul's theology reflected in Galatians and other letters became the justification of the oneness he believed all humanity now shared. In other words, his mission to the Gentiles was not because of his theology. His theology was because of that mission that had proven to be successful. It expanded his vision of God's people being the whole of humanity.

Based on reading Paul's views within the context of Judaism's communalism, his words do not support the concept of original sin that arose in the 5th century from the mind of St. Augustine, a bishop in North Africa. Augustine interpreted the story of Adam and Eve literally, historicizing a Jewish midrash, a story, not an actual event. Their disobedience in the Garden of Eden infected the whole of the human race which is why, Augustine supposed, he himself gave in to his carnal desires before becoming Christian. He likely found comfort in Paul's confession in his letter to the Christians in Rome:

> I do not understand my own actions. For I do not do what I want, but I do the very thing I hate.[16] Now if I do what I do not want, I agree that the law is good.[17] But in fact it is no longer I who do it but sin that dwells within me.[18] For I know that the good does not dwell within me, that is, in my flesh. For the desire to do the good lies close at hand, but not the ability.[19] For I do not do the good I want, but the evil I do not want is what I do.[20] Now if I do what I do not want, it is no longer I who do it but sin that dwells within me. (Romans 7:15-20)

Who doesn't find solace in the notion that there is a force ("evil") inside of us that drives us to do things we don't even want to do. But nothing in this text or any other suggests Paul believed in anything like "original sin." He believed Adam represented human life in the flesh and Jesus represented human life in the spirit. (1 Corinthians 15:45-49)

But let's not get bogged down in text analysis, but focus on the larger point that the nature of God is why original sin represents a theological tangent that led Christianity to elevate divine punishment above divine love. Nothing, for example, in Hebrew scripture even hints that God abandoned covenant with the people of Israel. The Deuteronomic ethic of blessings and curses that was written early in Israel's history was later rejected as the Book of Job tells us. Jeremiah says that God renewed the covenant by writing it on the people's hearts. (31:31-34) How did that God suddenly become vindictive, demanding recompense for sin without which the whole of humanity would be condemned? Interpreting Jesus' death on the cross as the means by which personal salvation became possible ultimately raises more questions than it can ever answer.

Also noteworthy for Christianity's own history is that theological diversity actually existed in the church before creedal Christianity took control of church teaching, something that receives less attention in the church than it should. A British theologian named Pelagius, for example, took issue with Augustine's concept of original sin, arguing that human beings were as morally responsible creatures quite capable of living right by choosing morality over immorality, truth over falsehood, the spirit over the flesh. The church obviously sided with Augustine through creedal formulations expressed most fully at the Councils of Carthage (411) and Orange (529) that openly affirmed the concept of original sin. In-between these councils the Council of Trent (403) added further explanation by declaring that humans "contracted sin rather than "committing" sin. That is, they declared that sin is a state of being rather than a willful act.

This is where things stand today, in spite of the fact that many scholars question the efficacy of the various concepts of atonement salvation the doctrine of original sin makes necessary. My position is that Christians need to see the whole concept of individual salvation as contradictory to believing in a God who is loving. More than that, the notion that a loving God would require a human sacrifice to be reconciled to humanity makes no sense. God created humanity in the first place with the freedom to think for ourselves, choose for ourselves, and the natural inclination for both good and evil. The creation story about the Garden of Eden was Judaism's way of saying that having free will meant that humans would make mistakes even in paradise, but that free will was the only way the divine/human relationship had meaning. Having no choice but to be good meant good had no meaning. The choice between good and evil is what gives either of them meaning.

Individualism has warped our view of humanity to the point where Christians need to affirm the centrality of community core to Judaism, born of the fundamental belief that God called a people, not a person, into covenant. Exodus tells us that the reason God led the people out of Egyptian slavery was because God saw "their suffering." (Exodus 3:7) Jesus called disciples. He didn't go it alone. The hope the people had in the messiah was the restoration of the nation of Israel, not individual salvation. That was a later development in Christian thinking much like the concept of a "second coming" that would fulfill the expectations the first coming failed to fulfill.

Interestingly, upon close examination the claim that Jesus' death made individual salvation is seen to be self-contradictory. If Jesus died for the sins of the world as traditional Christianity claims, the effect of his death is communal and individual salvation becomes unnecessary. Moreover, without the need for salvation, living a life that is pleasing to God, something Paul counseled Christians of his day to do (1 Corinthians 12:1-2) is the way you express gratitude to God for love and grace. You don't try to please God to get God's love or forgiveness. You try to please God because you are thankful for life itself. How you live matters more and understanding who Jesus was matters less. You know enough to follow his example, to listen to the wisdom of his teachings.

In this context, if we want to talk about salvation at all, the way it has any relevant meaning is that it is about being saved from a life less than what God created it to be, a life that is spiritually whole. That understanding is consistent with the Latin word for salvation (salvare) that means "to save," as does the Greek word soteria that means "deliverance from harm," and the Greek verb sózó which means to heal or to make whole. Salvation should be a way of talking about wholeness, healing, inclusion, not judgment because of our brokenness or justification for being in the presence of God or excluded from it. If God's love is forever unconditional, that is a promise that God will always be with us. No one is excluded from that love in this life or in the next. We may experience it differently, but the gift of life with God is communal, for all, not just for some. This is what heaven is, literally, the "abode" or dwelling place of God, where God is, which is everywhere. Thus, heaven is being in the presence of God, which has no beginning or end because God has no beginning or end. Our awareness of being in the presence of God depends on the degree of our spiritual sensitivity, but awareness does not affect the presence of God. God is present whether we know it or not.

The conclusion to which all of this leads is that unconditional divine love makes salvation redundant and, therefore, unnecessary. How we respond to God is our choice, but whatever we decide does not alter the fundamental claim that a loving God is with us, now and forever because God is God. What is more, the degree to which faith impacts our lives is determined by our capacity to trust that this image of God is true.

9

THE BREATH OF LIFE

The church has overlaid the Holy Spirit with Christian embellishment by making it the third person of the Trinity—God the Father, God the Son, God the Holy Spirit—that serves no purpose. If anything, it complicates the simple fact that both Judaism and Christianity use the words wind, breath, and spirit when speaking of God without any need to turn them into a confusing doctrine about the nature of God.

The Hebrew word ruach translates into English as spirit, breath, and wind. Ruach is "wind" as in Numbers 11:31 and Exodus 10:13, "spirit" as in Genesis 2:1, Judges 6:34, 1 Samuel 16:14, 1 Kings 18:12, while it is translated "breath" in texts such as Genesis 2:7 and Job 12:10. The phrase Ruach Elohim means Holy Spirit. (Genesis 41:39; Psalm 51:11) Spirit in whatever form is intended to convey the image of the presence, the work, the power of God to give life. In Greek, "pneuma" means "spirit" and also "power." All of these words are helpful in describing the ways God works in creation and human life. The image of God "breathing" life into human beings holds meaning because it suggests a fundamental connection with God beyond human weaknesses and frailties. Because God has breathed life into all of us, we are inseparably part of God and God is part of us.

These metaphorical references lose their power when they are literalized. The Holy Spirit is simply a metaphor for the presence of God. Making it into the third person of the Holy Trinity is a way of stating the obvious, that God's presence is real. Creating a doctrine literalizes mystery, something that has no evidence of achieving much more than a basis for controversy, exclusion, and division. Trying to explain mystery usually ends in explaining it away. That is the heart of the problem with trinitarian faith.

God is one God, or there is no God has always been the anchor point for my faith. Ministers have developed clever ways to explain the Trinity such as comparing it to water that has three forms—water, ice, and vapor. Makes sense except it says nothing helpful about God we don't already know. I don't recall ever needing or wanting to know if the Holy Spirit was of the same substance as God. The more important question is whether God is present and, if so, how, and the only way to know is through the eyes of faith. In turn, that becomes a matter of trusting God is real and present in the way you or I perceive to be the case. I am a minister today because I chose to trust I had experienced the presence of God in what the church says is a call to ministry when I had no evidence to prove it.

I vividly remember what happened. I was listening to someone reading 1 Corinthians 13 aloud, "the love chapter" as it is called, and when they finished I had this overwhelming thought that I should study for the ministry. It came out of nowhere. I had never thought about being a minister before that moment, but there it was. I was finishing my freshman year in college and had declared English as my major. I had not had any courses in religion. I went to church occasionally, but nothing more than that. I still believe that is what happened to me. I could describe it as God speaking to me in that moment, or I can say I had an overwhelming sense of the presence of God that was in the form of thinking I should become a minister. Nothing about the experience changes regardless of the words I use to describe it.

That is not all I can say about why I entered into ministry, but for all these years it has been enough. It is tempting to make more of a spiritual experience than is needed or helpful. Actually, it is often true that the more we say, the less credible the interpretation of it being of the Holy Spirit becomes. I think that is why "speaking in tongues" has such little credibility in the eyes of outside observers. I have witnessed it a few times in such a way that I was left thinking that it was for show instead of for God. Yet, I have also witnessed a clergy staff of a church with whom I was consulting engage in speaking in tongues during a weekend retreat that I would describe as gentle, beautiful, and genuine. Because anything we say about the Holy Spirit is a statement of faith about the mystery of God's presence, the less said the better. That someone would insist it is evidence of having been given a special gift of God's power causes me to think of hubris more than the Holy Spirit.

In Judaism, the Holy Spirit or Holy Ghost is a way to describe the power, force, or presence of God over the whole of creation. As we have said, Genesis says the spirit brought creation into existence and the breath of God gave life to human beings. (1:2; 2:7) Christians elevated spirit to "personhood" when the Nicene Creed articulated a God in three persons faith statement. I think the Jewish way was and remains adequate. Calling the presence of God the Holy Spirit doesn't change the reality to which it is referring. It is a witness of faith to believe God is present in human affairs. Being disciplined enough to say as little as possible beyond that helps. As I noted in the chapter about God, caution is always advisable when speaking about God.

It is amazing the difference the right choice of words can make. Saying, "I believe God was present" carries more credibility than making the declarative statement, "God was present." To say, "I believe God called me to ministry," is more credible than declaring that God called me. It may seem like a minor difference, but it is a minor difference that matters. The Jewish practice of speaking of God's presence without deifying spirit to Godhead status avoids being entangled in trinitarian doctrine that leads to theological confusion as is always the case when Christians cannot leave metaphors alone. It seems enough to speak of God as spirit in the same way as you speak of God as love. Spirit is presence. Holy Spirit is God's presence, a way of saying God is in all things, including those experiences in which we sense a presence beyond ourselves we call God. Nothing more need be said because in truth nothing more can be said.

10

THE BIBLE AND CULTURE WARS

The chapter on reading the Bible honestly raised numerous questions about the ways Christians use the Bible. In recent years one of those ways is to fuel what has come to be known as "culture wars." These are conflicts over moral issues conservative Christians, specifically, evangelicals, believe represent the growth of secular humanism and the decline of Christian influence in America. Whether that is true or not is a discussion for another day, but culture war issues are real and the Bible is frequently used to justify them, with varying levels of impact. If the issue is over manger scenes on a courthouse lawn, the impact is minimal even if seen as symbolically significant. It becomes another matter when the issue affects and influences the way other people are treated, especially when laws are passed that attempt to legislate morality.

The two issues that are the most prominent in this regard are homosexuality and abortion. Evangelical Christians believe both are sins, violations or transgressions against God's moral laws. More than that, they believe a society that accepts homosexual behavior and/or allows abortion will be harshly judged by God for doing so. Rigidity characterizes their position on both issues. For evangelicals, each is an example of a betrayal of America's enduring Christian foundations.

Are they right? Is there a more balanced perspective that reflects a more sensible and sensitive approach to abortion and homosexuality? Does reading the Bible honestly expose the evangelical practice of misusing scripture on both issues? I believe the answer is yes to both questions. Let me explain why.

The first thing an honest reading of the Bible reveals is that the word "abortion" does not appear in either the Hebrew Bible or the New Testament. The Bible says nothing directly about abortion, which means using scripture to support views on either side of the issue can only be done by inference. That makes claims about what the Bible says purely subjective. Genesis 9:6, for example, says, "Whoever sheds the blood of a human, by a human shall that person's blood be shed; for in his own image God made humankind," is interpreted as a statement against abortion, but the text itself gives no indication the writer(s) was talking about a pregnant woman.

Another passage often cited is Exodus 21:22-25:

> When people who are fighting injure a pregnant woman so that there is a miscarriage, and yet no further harm follows, the one responsible shall be fined what the woman's husband demands, paying as much as the judges determine. If any harm follows, then you shall give life for life, eye for eye, tooth for tooth, hand for hand, foot for foot, burn for burn, wound for wound, stripe for stripe.

The irony of evangelicals using this text is that it actually suggests the mother's life is valued more than the life of the fetus. If the latter dies, the text says, the perpetrator must pay the woman's husband whatever he demands, but it goes on to say that if the woman suffers further harm, the perpetrator's punishment is to suffer reciprocal harm, possibly including a life for life. It's beside the point, though, because the text offers no substantive guidance regarding the divisions around abortion today.

In addition, Judaism has always held to the position that life begins at birth, not inception. In an article entitled, "The Beginning of Life in Judaism," Dr. Fred Rosner, Professor of Medicine at New York's Mount Sinai School of Medicine, explains that Judaism has always taught that life begins at birth, not conception, and even then the infant does not reach the full status of a person for thirty days afterwards.

The Talmud states in part that if the "greater part was already born, one may not touch it, for one may not set aside one person's life for that of another." Thus the act of birth changes the status of the fetus from a nonperson to a person (nefesh). Killing the newborn after this point is infanticide. Many Talmudic sources and commentators on the Talmud substitute the word "head" for "greater part." Others maintain the "greater part" verbatim. Maimonides and Joseph Caro also consider the extrusion of the head to indicate birth. They both further state that by rabbinic decree, even if only one limb of the fetus was extruded and then retracted, childbirth is considered to have occurred.

Rosner goes on to say:

Not only is the precise time of the birth of paramount importance in adjudicating whether aborting the fetus is permissible to save the mother's life, but the viability of the fetus must also be taken into account. The newborn child is not considered fully viable until it has survived thirty days following birth, as is stated in the Talmud...Thus, although the newborn infant reaches the status of a person or nefesh, which it didn't have prior to birth, it still does not enjoy all the legal rights of an adult until it has survived for thirty days postpartum.[52]

While it is unlikely that abortion opponents will be influenced by the Jewish view of when life begins, the clarification is important nonetheless, not least because using Hebrew scripture to justify laws that ban abortion choice for women represents using Jewish scripture without regard for what texts mean to Jews. An honest reading of the Bible leads to the unequivocal conclusion that abortion choice opponents are not basing their belief on what scripture actually says. That doesn't make their views wrong or invalid, only that they are engaged in proof texting when they use the Bible to support what they already believe. If you remember, this is what Novella calls the logical fallacy of confirmation bias and motivated reasoning.

What is truly ironic, though, about today's debate over abortion is that abortion itself is the secondary issue in this culture war conflict. The primary one has to do with who gets to choose whether or not to have an abortion. There are women who would never have an abortion except in the case of rape, incest, or their own life being in jeopardy, but who also believe women in consultation with their doctor should be the ones to make the decision, no one else. Evangelicals reject this position because they believe they are being a voice for the unborn. When you think about it, that is a rather arrogant position to take because it is de facto saying that women facing these circumstances give no thought to their own fetus.

Choice, then, is the issue, and Christians who want laws passed to ban abortion options insist that politicians, most of whom are male, who have no idea what the experience of pregnancy is like, should be the ones to decide. When the Supreme Court struck down Roe v. Wade in 2022, it gave state legislatures the right to insert themselves in this way. In a real sense, the Court decided that this most personal decision a woman can ever make is actually a states-rights issue that supersedes the personal nature of the situation.

None of this is to say that advocates for a woman's right to choose cannot fall into extremism as well. The argument that there should be no restrictions on abortion rights represents such a view. Yet, not even Roe v. Wade took this position. It in fact acknowledged the need for balance among the various sides in order to reach a compromise that respects different views. Writing for the majority, Justice Harry Blackmun said as much in the opening paragraphs of the decision:

> We forthwith acknowledge our awareness of the sensitive and emotional nature of the abortion controversy, of the vigorous opposing views, even among physicians, and of the deep and seemingly absolute convictions that the subject inspires. One's philosophy, one's experiences, one's exposure to the raw edges of human existence, one's religious training, one's attitudes toward life and family and their values, and the moral standards one establishes and seeks to observe,

are all likely to influence and to color one's thinking and conclusions about abortion.

The decision they reached stated that "a person may choose to have an abortion until a fetus becomes viable, based on the right to privacy contained in the Due Process Clause of the Fourteenth Amendment. Viability means the ability to live outside the womb, which usually happens between 24 and 28 weeks after conception." They also said that at the point of viability, the compelling interests of the state may lead to further restrictions so long as they don't violate or restrict the rights set forth by Roe.

In this way Roe v. Wade was a compromise that affirmed both a woman's right to choose and the state's right of compelling interests in the well-being of the fetus, both with reasonable limitations. Yet, it was an unacceptable compromise for evangelical Christians whose views were and remain set in stone, in my judgment precisely because they refuse to read the Bible honestly. The conservative majority Supreme Court decision in 2022 also rejected the compromise of the 1973 decision and turned the matter over to the states as if a woman's personal rights were subject to state interpretation. By that standard no black southerner would have achieved full citizenship, the right to vote, or equal opportunity in housing or employment when they did, and in some instances could still be seeking some if not all of them.

Complicating the divisions over abortion today is the fact that the basis for the Catholic Church's position on abortion is less biblical and more ecclesial than is the case with Protestant evangelicals. For Catholics the prohibition on abortion rights is a church teaching. Reading the Bible honestly has less bearing on the Catholic position than church dogma whose authority depends solely on what the church says. Yet, all Catholic church teaching is as equally subjective as Protestant interpretations of the Bible. When the church speaks, Catholics are to listen, but they are listening to the voices of men who may believe they are speaking for God, but who in truth are speaking as fallible, flawed human beings.

It seems to me that there is no path forward on the matter of a woman's right to choose for Christianity unless and until both sides are willing to accept compromise as the tool for progress. States such as South Carolina, South Dakota, Tennessee, Texas, Kentucky, Louisiana, and Missouri that make no exceptions for rape or incest show no sign of being willing to find middle ground. It seems to me that the only possibility for common ground depends on the willingness of evangelical Christians to do so rather than lobbying politicians to enact severe abortion laws. That would involve Protestant evangelicals and Catholic hierarchy acknowledging that what they think, how they interpret scripture, and what they believe about divine moral law are always subjective perceptions of human beings who seek to do God's will without knowing it perfectly. It would also mean that pro-choice advocates recognize that no right is absolute, subject as all rights are by circumstances and new information.

Practically, in this instance compromise means reestablishing Roe v. Wade as the law of the land unless and until medical science discovers more about gestational development and fetal viability than we now know. In addition, no position or political policy should ever be set in concrete precisely because research constantly yields new information no one can anticipate and certainly should not ignore. Until a commitment to political compromise on abortion is understood as essential as it is on all other political issues, it seems likely divisions in the church and in the nation over this issue will not soon pass, even if one side or the other prevails politically.

In regard to homosexuality, evangelicals are no more inclined to engage in compromise than they are on a woman's right to choose.[53] They insist that it is a behavior, not an orientation, that goes against what the Bible says about it. Not only did they oppose the Supreme Court decision in 2015 to legalize gay marriage, they believe it made matters worse because the Bible says marriage is a union between a man and a woman. But the evangelical perspective about homosexuality ignores research that has confirmed that genetics plays a role in sexual orientation. A very large recent study, for example, concluded that while there is no "gay gene" that determines sexual orientation, genetics do influence sexual orientation much as they do in other human traits.[54] "The message should remain the same [as previous studies]," says one of the leaders of the study, "that this is a complex behavior that genetics definitely plays a part in."[55] A report on the study published in the online journal "Science" by Joycelyn Kaiser concluded, "When the researchers combined all the variants they measured across the entire genome, they estimate that genetics can explain between 8% and 25% of non-heterosexual behavior. The rest, they say, is explained by environmental influences, which could range from hormone exposure in the womb to social influences later in life."[56]

Biblical writers, of course, knew nothing of genetics. Their views about homosexuality were limited by their time in history and should not be considered binding on later generations as if advancements in scientific research don't matter. Also, incredibly important are the personal experiences gay and lesbian individuals have begun to share that shed light on who they are. I have personally heard numerous stories gay and lesbian Christians have told that belie any suggestion that they have chosen to live a gay life-style they could choose to give up if they wanted to. More than a few have said they initially denied their orientation to themselves. Others went through family rejection when they came out, but had no thought of "giving-up" being gay as their family urged them to do. But the critical point is that because genetics is without question a factor in a person's sexual orientation, labeling it a "sin" becomes meaningless and can become a form of spiritual abuse.

I grew up at a time when homosexuals were labeled "sick" people, and the American Psychiatric Association labeled it a mental disorder. It was not until 1973 that the A.P.A. changed its position, and even then its resolution was considered ambiguous by many gays and lesbians. Responding to criticisms of it, Dr. Robert L. Spitzer, who at the time was a psychiatrist at the Columbia College of Physicians and Surgeons, said: "We're not saying that homosexuality is either normal or 'abnormal.'"[57] Since then both the field of psychiatry and the country as a whole have grown past its fears and prejudices leading to an opening of personal, professional, and even religious doors to gay and lesbian men and women that were once closed. As long as evangelicals persist in living in the past as if new knowledge makes no difference to what they believe, they will continue to do harm to people whose sexual orientation they refuse to understand.

Overall, then, there is no biblical reason to call abortion "murder" and homosexuality an "abomination" before God. These are intentionally emotionally charged labels that make compromise between religion and state on these issues less likely when that is the only way to end conflict between them. The path for evangelicals—and all Christians actually—that combines faithfulness and wisdom is compromise. Moreover, I learned from my own mother that it is not as difficult to find as it may seem.

At the age of 93 she finally agreed to give up living alone and moved to North Carolina to live with my brother and his wife. Soon thereafter, but prior to the Supreme Court ruling on gay marriage, evangelicals in the state managed to persuade the Republican controlled legislature to seek public approval of a referendum that banned gay marriage. It passed and then was nullified by the Supreme Court ruling. Soon after the referendum passed, though, my wife and I were visiting our Carolina family. At dinner one evening I asked Mother how she voted on the referendum. I confess that I did so because I knew she was opposed to gay marriage and wanted to talk to her again as we had done before about why she felt the way she did. She shocked all of us when she said without hesitation, "I voted against it." Stunned, I said incredulously, "You voted against it? But you don't believe in gay marriage." "I know I don't," she replied, "but I don't think I have the right to tell somebody else who they can marry."

I think that is what blending wisdom and faithfulness looks like, and it is the most sensible way for American Christians today to help bring people closer together on issues that are being exploited by politicians and religious zealots to separate them. Gay marriage is now the law of the land and in every state where a woman's right to choose has been on the ballot, it has won. There is no ambiguity about where most Americans stand on both issues. They don't want restrictions on what they see as an issue of personal freedom imposed on them by politicians trying to legislate morality.

Culture wars over either puts beliefs above relationships. That is why culture wars are lost before they even get started. A free-thinking people will always refuse to be told what they must believe and how they must live when it comes to anything they interpret as moralistic or suppressing their personal freedom. Empirically we know that Americans today are quite capable of holding on to universal values that Christians also embrace and at the same time resist personal moral views being forced on them. When it comes to abortion and homosexuality, a Christianity of the future must realize that efforts to legislate personal morality have never worked lest it proves that those who do not learn from the mistakes of the past are doomed to repeat them.[58]

The Christian community should be a safe place for women who face a decision about having an abortion or have had one. Nor is it right to exclude anyone because of their sexual orientation. Not even acceptance is enough. They should be welcomed and embraced. The gay and lesbian couples who were members of the church Joy and I started were not looking for a "gay" church. They said they were looking for a church whose message was that everyone belongs to God, loved by God, everyone is not only a neighbor, but a sister and brother. All the church has to be is church for that to be their experience.

A Christianity of the future will also need to end culture wars in general that are undermining both itself and the internal cohesiveness American society needs to survive. Here is where it needs to follow the lead of Christian skeptics who know how to balance what we know with what we don't know about abortion, homosexuality, and all other culture war issues. Skepticism offers a check on outrageous claims often made to score political points that fuel passions, but shed no light on facts. The assertion that a fetus is a person making all abortions murder, for example, is one a skeptical mind would challenge as being without medical evidence or biblical support, thus, adding nothing helpful in finding common ground.

Christian skeptics also serve as a model for being willing to live with ambiguity. It is the reason skepticism plays such a vital role in the pursuit of truth. Research offers guidance, but has not led to definitive facts that can answer all questions on either subject. Because medical science is evolving, ambiguity is a fact of life on these and other issues, making skepticism an essential tool to get at the best truth we can discern. At the end of the day, finding common ground on controversial issues like abortion and homosexuality needs a healthy dose of humility that skepticism helps make possible as we work to build a better world rather than to tear it down because we didn't get our way.

11

COMMUNITY RATHER THAN CONFORMITY

If Christianity in America isn't in free fall, "it's damn close to it," to quote words the late conservative Arizona Senator Barry Goldwater often used to make a point. On several occasions I have suggested both American churches and American Christianity are in trouble. It is now time to provide the statistics that support that concern.

While the United States is not and never has been a Christian nation, it is and always has been a nation of Christians. Ninety percent of all Americans were Christians when the nation was founded, a figure that remained relatively stable until around 1990. That's when the percentage began to decline, dropping to 64% by 2020. The Pew Research Center says that if current trends continue, by 2070 Christians will make up less than 50% of the population for the first time in our nation's history.[59] These results led Daniel Silliman to write in the conservative journal, Christianity Today, "If you're trying to predict the future religious landscape in America, according to Pew, the question is not whether Christianity will decline. It's how fast and how far."[60]

This situation follows a precipitous decline in both church attendance and membership that began in the 1960s. Relatively few people now attend church on any regular basis, somewhere around 25%. A recent newspaper column suggests the situation is worse than that: "Although 21% to 24% of us say we attend services regularly, research tracking people's actual behavior shows that, in fact, the number may be as small as 5%, or 1 person in 20. Worse, the 5% statistic is based on research conducted before the COVID-19 pandemic devastated religious attendance even further."[61] Apparently, the best we can say is that 75% of Americans don't attend church at all or only occasionally, usually Christmas and Easter. What is more, the percentage of Americans still holding church membership now stands at 46%.[62]

The troubles in the church and their effects on Christianity are also having an impact on clergy who are under stress and are feeling discouraged. In 2015, 72 percent of pastors reported feeling "very satisfied" with their jobs. Five years later that percentage had dipped to 67 percent, and then the bottom fell out in 2022 when only 52 percent said they felt "very satisfied" with their ministry.[63] Seminary enrollment has also been trending downward for several years. Many schools have sold their campuses and now rent office space for a reduced faculty and staff and limited classroom courses. Some are renting the buildings they once owned.

A twist in this tale of woes for the church and Christianity is that the people leaving Christianity are Christians. Think about that. Christians not only don't want to be in church or become an ordained minister anymore. They don't want to be identified with Christianity, a faith tradition in which many of them were raised. That is an astonishing development. These are not "godless secularists," people who want to tear down Christianity, people who have turned away from God. They are people of faith, often the children of the church, maybe even your own children, or grandchildren. Some of them are in fact parents and grandparents themselves who have spent their lives in the church. Now they have left both the church and Christianity.

Something is seriously wrong in the Christian community. Put starkly, large numbers of Christians don't like Christianity anymore, at least not the kind they see today. It's like having friends tell you they don't want to be around you anymore. It may be because of things you say, your attitude about other people or groups of people, or they don't like the fact that you talk and act as if your views are the only views, or the only ones that matter.

Whatever the reason, the message should be clear. You're losing the very people who used to want to be around you. Exacerbating what is happening is that many of the people whose words and actions are the cause seem oblivious to the negative impact they are having.

In 2024, for example, at the urging of evangelical Christians, the Louisiana state legislature passed a law requiring the Ten Commandments to be posted in every public school. One of the co-sponsors of the bill was a woman legislator who cited the nation's moral decline as justification for the new law. Offering support for her bill, Louisiana Governor Jeff Landry remarked, "This country was founded on Judeo Christian principles, and every time we steer away from that, we have problems in our nation."[64]

As of this writing, the law's constitutionality is, of course, under challenge, but the picture it paints is of Christians straining at a gnat and swallowing a camel, given the fact that Louisiana has the fourth lowest literacy rate in the nation, with over 25% of its citizens unable to read or write, and is ranked second only to Mississippi in the number of people living below the national poverty line.[65] Yet the state legislature is spending its time trying to legislate morality.

Whatever the motivation evangelical Christians have for these kinds of actions, they are painting an image of Christianity that is decidedly negative. It's not a new problem, of course. It was reflected in the 1971 John Lennon song "Imagine" whose lyrics included the words:

> Imagine there's no countries
> It isn't hard to do
> Nothing to kill or die for
> And no religion, too

The song has become an iconic peace sung around the world, including being used in the 2024 Paris Olympic Games. And each time it is sung the message being inculcated in the minds of those listening is that religion is a source of conflict the world would be better without. The tragedy is that Christianity is better than this image when it abandons its rigidity of beliefs that inevitably produces conflict and division, focusing instead on being in the world the way Jesus was. Franciscan priest Richard Rohr puts it this way:

> Christianity is a lifestyle, a way of being in the world that is simple, non-violent, shared, and loving. However, we made it into an established 'religion' (and all that goes with that) and avoided the lifestyle change itself. One could be warlike, greedy, racist, selfish, and vain in most of Christian history, and still believe that Jesus is one's "personal Lord and Savior" ... The world has no time for such silliness anymore. The suffering on Earth is too great.[66]

Not only does the world not have time for the "silliness" Rohr says contradicts how Christians are supposed to be in the world, neither does Christianity. In Greek the word "silliness" ("anoisia") means "nonsense." Christianity as an organized religion defined by rigid beliefs may not be "nonsense," but it has gotten close to it because a lot of what churches believe makes right living harder instead of better. According to Jesus, right living is not complicated. "I give you a new commandment," he said to his disciples, "that you love one another. Just as I have loved you, you also should love one another." (John 13:34-35) That is what right living means, loving one another, loving your neighbor, even your enemies, as we have said. It's not complicated, except the church has overlaid the message of Jesus with an insistence on believing the right things the church says Christians must believe. As a result, conformity is valued over community.

Today most people think being a church member, indeed, being a Christian, means you believe certain things, mostly about Jesus. They do because that is what the church has been saying for centuries. The argument was that conformity to right beliefs protected the gospel from theological corruption, but in truth conformity has always been about protecting church authority which quickly led to serving the interest of institutional perpetuation. Actually, the church's demand for conformity of beliefs worked for many centuries, perhaps a testimony to the power or exploitation of divine sanction as the church cloaked its teachings and declaration as being sanctioned by God.

But it also produced conflicts that led countries into wars that continued until the 1648 Treaty of Westphalia ending the Thirty-Years War and breaking the back of the Holy Roman Empire. German princes gained the freedom to choose the religion of their fiefdoms, whether Catholic or Protestant. Religious persecution continued, of course, even with the wars at an end, which eventually led to the colonists coming to America to escape religious persecution. Unwilling to learn from history and, thus, repeating its mistakes, John Winthrop lead a break-away group of Puritans to found the Massachusetts Bay Colony modeled on "God's law" and the Anglican Church doctrine and practices. The legacy of Puritanism is of an oppressive Christianity whose rigidity and self-righteous judgmentalism led to its own end.

But New England Puritanism was not the only form of Christian hegemony in America. One of the worst examples of learning nothing from history and then repeating it was my native Virginia. Ignoring the history of conflict caused by the mixing of church and state in Europe, in the year 1619 the House of Burgesses officially designated the Church of England as the established church of the Colony. That did not change officially until Thomas Jefferson and James Madison managed to get the Virginia Statute for Religious Freedom adopted in 1786 which became the basis for the First Amendment.

This change meant churches were forced to perpetuate themselves through voluntary funding. Numerical growth served this need. More members meant more money in the offering plate. Membership size and tangentially the size of the budget became the primary measures of success. This history serves as the backdrop to the connection between conformity of beliefs and institutional perpetuation. Once the church was without the authority of the state in the European model of collusion of church and state, churches were forced to find another way to maintain themselves. The Catholic Church had been doing it through conformity of beliefs since the beginning of Christianity. Protestant churches struggled to do so because of individual freedom of belief and practice that was endemic to the

Protestant movement as a whole. Puritanism sought to impose its beliefs through civil regulations and laws, but failed. Since then American Protestant churches have struggled to find ways to support individual freedom of thought and at the same time promote the authority of the Bible.

The framers of the Constitution were familiar with this history and ingeniously established a religiously neutral form of self-government that allowed for religious freedom while excluding any form of conformity of religious beliefs. Sects and denominations within American Christianity have had varying degrees of difficulty in coping with the institutional separation of church and state the Constitution demands. Social mores born of leftover Puritan attitudes and beliefs maintained a degree of wide-spread conformity to Christian practices and beliefs until individual freedom asserted itself on a large scale with the civil unrest of the 1960s that led to the questioning of all authority, including that of the government itself. It is not coincidental that the decline in church attendance began in the mid-1960s.

Remnants of the past still remain in evangelical congregations where conformity of beliefs is the reason they view skepticism as an enemy of faith. Through the use of the fear of divine judgment, evangelical preachers have created an environment in which the pressure to conform to establish norms of belief has been so forceful that it has produced a kind of evangelical groupthink, a term first introduced by psychologist Irving Janis who conducted extensive research on group decision-making by people under conditions of stress.[67] What he observed is that under overt or perceived pressure, people suppress their own doubts and questions in order to accept group decisions, similar to what we today describe as going along to get along. They may suppress their own concerns even when they are troubled by the potential ethical and moral consequences of the group's decisions.

That is how evangelical congregations function today. Church members suppress their doubts and questions in order to support the mission of their congregation to convert the world to Christianity, as if that is the will of God, especially here in America. As such, they wittingly or unwittingly focus attention on what Harvard scholar Robert Putnam described several years ago as bonding that reinforces exclusive identities within homogeneous groups," in contrast to bridging that encompasses people across diverse social cleavages.[68]

Groups can do both, but when bonding becomes their primary goal they can turn inward and become exclusivist. It's what happens when the demand for conformity is strong enough to diminish diversity that is essential for Christian community that is inherently inclusive. Genuine community exists when inclusion, voluntary participation, and the welcoming of diversity and differences are valued. These in turn create the bonding Putnam says members of groups, especially faith communities, experience. Healthy faith communities also seek to engage in bridging that expands the reach of belonging to encompass those who would otherwise be left outside the circle of inclusion.

One of the gifts of genuine community is that individuals don't have to disappear to be part of it which indirectly makes space for skepticism that contributes to the healthiness of the community. Community does not seek to hide, ignore, or diminish individualism. It calls it to go beyond itself to avoid selfishness and self-centeredness. Community saves individualism from isolationism produced by radical individualism. Christian community provides a place to experience the truth that we are made for each other. This is why an exclusive church for any reason, and certainly because of an insistence on conformity of beliefs, is an oxymoron. An exclusive church is not church. It is a church, an organization, an institution, but it is not church. Being church means community.

In spite of the fact that the church is and always has been made up of human beings, not gods, not angels, just ordinary people with feet of clay like everyone else, genuine community is possible when there is no expectation or demand for conformity of belief. I know this to be the case because of my own experience growing up in a denomination whose founders chose unity over uniformity, rejecting the use of creedal statements of faith as unavoidably divisive. They did so because of the history of Protestant divisions in the Scottish Presbyterian tradition of which they were a part. They believed community was possible only in the context of unity, and unity was possible when the only demand to be Christian was to confess Jesus as Lord and commit yourself to following his way of life based in your own understanding of scripture. I learned from my church that diversity was a good thing, whether theological, social, or racial. Individual congregations have not always embraced diversity, but they have nonetheless valued freedom of thought above conformity.

My denomination did not, of course, avoid the trappings of institutionalism and so has been weighed down as all the others have with an excessive bureaucracy and organizational heaviness that have been and are obstacles to both bonding and bridging. Moreover, informal and unofficial expectations for conformity exist in the form of pressure to be a "team player." Yet, the ideal of Christian unity without uniformity has remained bedrock to our identify and limited the impact any expressions of conformity have taken. We often marvel among ourselves that after nearly two-hundred years there is a sense of connectedness among clergy and congregations that has actually increased as we have suffered from decline in the same way other denominations have. Nor is it surprising to us that we have witnessed an acceptance of gay and lesbian Christians into membership and into ordained ministry, not without controversy, but without major divisions.

I don't tell this story to pedestalize my denomination as the ideal. Even to suggest that would be dishonest and disingenuous. I share my own journey only to highlight the fact that the bonding that instills a strong sense of identity without any demand for conformity of beliefs both theological and moral is possible within a community that is intentionally inclusive and diverse.

The need and challenge is for Christians to engage in the work of building community. That is not only essential for the vitality of Christianity in today's world. Robert Putnam whom I mentioned earlier, argues that the nation needs strong faith communities to help build social capital he defines as "connections among individuals—social networks and the norms of reciprocity and trustworthiness that arise from them." Social capital, he further says, "calls attention to the fact that social virtue is most powerful when it is embedded in a dense network of reciprocal social relations." Describing community as "the conceptual cousin to social capital," he highlights the fact that structured institutions enhance the civic life beyond those communities.[69]

Putnam believes faith communities are essential in the rebuilding of the declining social capital our nation has experienced that has produced social isolation and a break down in social cohesion. "It is hard to see," he writes, "how we could redress the erosion of the last several decades without a major religious contribution."[70] The need is urgent even, Putnam believes, because of the negative impact the decline of social capital has had on the physical and mental health of Americans.[71]

If churches want to be faith communities that contribute to the nation's social capital, they will need to maneuver through or around the claims of those within them who insist beliefs are what make someone a Christian. I suggest that the way for Christians to build genuine community without relying on efforts to force conformity of beliefs is to recover the power of thinking of ourselves as "followers of the way" as the first Christians were known (Acts 22:4, 24:14) rather than the modern identity of "believers" by which we are known. Following the way of Jesus is a radically different way of thinking of ourselves than being believers. One of the reasons the latter has taken root is because people have paid no attention to the way words shape and influence the way we see ourselves. We know a child's self-identity can be influenced by the names he is called. She unconsciously becomes who she is seen by others to be.

The same holds true for religious identity. To be called "believers" has taught generations of people that their Christian identity is determined by what they believe. If, on the other hand, Christians were called "followers of the way," their identity would be defined by what they do, how they live. It's such a simple, yet profound change because it shifts attention to behavior, to actions, to values, to a particular way of being in the world. It is also consistent with Jesus' call to be a loving person who must work at how to be such a person to both neighbors and enemies.

This focus on following Jesus highlights the need for living Christian in today's world, work that cannot and should not be done alone. The role of community is indispensable in being Christian. Conformity of any kind, but especially of beliefs, cannot create genuine community that is a by-product of unconditional love that celebrates the richness of diversity inclusion makes possible. Community is a place where people feel safe in being who they are. But I think one of the reasons churches struggle with being real communities of faith is because we idealize what that means. Community does not mean you like everybody who's a part of it. It doesn't mean you are friends with everyone. Community is much simpler than that. It is about having shared values. For Christians that means being committed to the value of devotion to God and the value of loving your neighbor as you love yourself. The second commandment necessarily includes the value of loving yourself since that determines the degree to which you love others.

It will take work in figuring out all the ways a community of faith embodies both of these values, but doing so is what the community must spend its time, energy, and resources doing. Everything else is extra, sometimes good and even fun, but always tangential and never central. Immediately you can see that creating this kind of Christian could challenge most churches that have made fellowship and activities that meet their needs core to their life together. Communities that are followers of the way have a different focus. They know that given the idolatries of modern life that demand devotion, equipping Christians to resist giving themselves more to those demands than to serving God through diverse ministries is not easy. But it is all that matters, and without which nothing else a church does will matter at all.

The most tell-tale sign of churches being communities of followers of the way is the degree to which inclusivity and diversity are priorities. They are two sides of the same coin. An inclusive community will be a diverse community. A diverse community will be an inclusive community. And for people of faith, both are signs of the presence of God. At this point, no one can predict the impact choosing community over conformity will have on the future of Christianity in America. But what we can know is that being people who embody the teachings of Jesus in how we live is the work we can and must do to make the world better. In truth, that is all we can do, and because of faith we can trust it is enough.

12

WORKING OUT YOUR OWN SALVATION

One of my least favorite phrases is, "Don't let the perfect be the enemy of the good." For most of my life I have considered it a justification for watering down change to the point of it being another name for maintaining the status quo. But years of being a church leader have taught me that when it comes to spiritual development, the perfect can indeed become the enemy of the good. An unreasonable standard for spiritual growth can lead to a rejection of progress that is not perfect, but is certainly good. And good is "good." The first story of creation in Genesis 1 that describes the seven days of creation ends with the words, "God saw everything that he had made, and indeed, it was very good." (Genesis 1: 31) "Very good" (tov me'od) underscores how good creation is. It is more than okay or acceptable. It is very good, outstanding even.

The Hebrew word for good (tov) has a variety of meanings, one of which is, "being as it should be." In other words, when something is good, it is what it should be. When you think about your own life in that way, being good would mean your life is as it should be. If you do something good, what you did is as it should be. Striving for good means to work at living as you should live, making your life what it should be. Just as the creation was as it should be at the moment of creation, so can your life be as you create it day to day.

...e to being good in the sense we are talking ...amental to it, is having personal integrity, ...eing "pure in heart." (Matthew 5:8) The Greek ... (katharos) means "unmixed" or "single-minded." ... a good word for single-mindedness. No ulterior ... intent to deceive. "Create in me a clean heart, O ... e plea in the song of David (Psalm 51:10), a plea to h... un-equivocating heart, one that is single-minded. When that singlemindedness is focused on living by the teachings of Jesus it leads to a "good" life, one in which you don't lose sight of the moral line that separates being who you are intended to be and not being that person. It is a life that doesn't damage your own soul, which is always a consequence of living without integrity. You can build a meaningful, purposeful, life on personal integrity. It is the essential, foundational quality of a good life.

The good news, then, is that being Christian means being the good person you were created to be. The bad news is that being Christian means being the good person you were intended to be. It doesn't just happen or fall from heaven. Just the opposite. Anyone who chooses to be Christian in the real world faces circumstances and influences that represent the opposite kind of values. Goodness doesn't come naturally any more than evil does. Judaism teaches that we are born with both inclinations and we have to choose which one will shape our lives.

I wonder if the Apostle Paul had this in mind when he wrote, "Therefore, my beloved, just as you have always obeyed me, not only in my presence, but much more now in my absence, work out your own salvation with fear and trembling." (Philippians 2:12) It's a strange phrasing from someone who interpreted the death of Jesus on the cross as God's gift of salvation. The key to understanding what he was saying may lie in the preceding verses in which he talks about living a self-less life, empty of conceit, humble and obedient to the will of God as Jesus did. From this perspective, working out your own salvation (soteria) means doing the hard work that empowers you to live your life the way it was intended to be lived.

Doing this kind of spiritual work that is devoted to living a good life, to being good, is precisely what a Christian skeptic should expect. One of the by-products of embracing the life of a Christian skeptic is accepting responsibility for yourself in every way, including growing into spiritual maturity. Working out your own salvation doesn't happen on its own. It takes work. When our granddaughter finished her first year of college and was getting ready to return home for the summer, she made the comment that while her freshman year had been great, she was anxious to be home again. In college, she said, you don't have anybody looking out for you. You have to do it yourself.

Without intending to she described how anyone achieves spiritual maturity. You have to do it yourself. Initially, I think most Christians want it that way, but they also discover that genuine commitment to the spiritual disciplines necessary to achieve this end can easily wane over time. As such, the natural question is what does that involve? As you would expect, there are numerous answers to the question, largely shaped by the experience of the person offering them. But there are some things enough people have found helpful that we can assume they can work for anyone who takes them seriously.

The most basic of all disciplines that I learned from the most mature Christians I have known, the women and men I call good people, is practicing the presence of God. To believe in God is also to believe God is present in the whole of life, that God is not distant, but as close as the air we breathe. While that is a statement of faith, it also reflects the experience many Christians have, including myself. I shared one of them in the story of my experience of being called to ministry. I have also experienced what I believe was the presence of God in moments of devotional reading of scripture such as the comfort I found reading the words, "Weeping may linger for the night, but joy comes with the morning" (Psalm 30:5) at the time of my brother's untimely death. Nothing else in the Psalm spoke to me except this one verse. It was the word I needed to hear at that moment, a moment I can only describe as experiencing the presence of God.

Henri Nouwen was convinced that one of the most obvious ways people of faith could experience the presence of God is what he described as "thinking in the presence of God." This is how he interpreted the Apostle Paul's words, "Rejoice always, pray without ceasing, give thanks in all circumstances, for this is the will of God in Christ Jesus for you." (1 Thessalonians 5:16-17) Nouwen said that initially the phrase, "pray without ceasing," made no sense to him, given that it seemed to be an impossible admonition. No one can pray without ceasing, just as no one can always rejoice, or give thanks all the time. He finally realized that what he did do all the time was to think. Thinking was as natural as breathing, leading Nouwen to believe that what praying without ceasing meant was to "think in the presence of God." He realized he could be conscious of God to such a degree that it would be the equivalent of constantly offering a prayer. In his own words:

> To pray, I think, does not mean to think about God in contrast to thinking about other things, nor does it mean spending time with God instead of spending time with other people. As soon as we begin to divide our thoughts into thoughts about God and thoughts about other things, like people and events, we separate God from our daily life. At that point God is allocated to a pious little niche in some corner of our lives where we only think pious thoughts and experience pious feelings. Although it is important and even indispensable for our spiritual lives to set apart time for God and God alone, our prayer can only become unceasing [prayer] when all our thoughts—beautiful or ugly, high or low, proud or shameful, sorrowful or joyful—can be thought in the presence of the One who dwells in us and surrounds us. By trying to do this, our unceasing thinking is converted into unceasing prayer, moving us from a self-centered monologue to a God-centered dialogue. To do this we want to try to convert our thoughts into conversation. The main question, therefore, is not so much what we think, but to whom we present our thoughts.[72]

A Muslim friend once explained the purpose of the five daily prayers of Islam in a similar way. Their intent, he said, was to make him conscious of the presence of Allah all the time so he would realize that every minute of his life was being lived in the presence of Allah. Some days he was very conscious of Allah, to the point where he did not need to follow the five prayers discipline. In being so conscious of Allah, he was already praying.

Thinking in the presence of God, being conscious of God regularly, is, then, a form of practicing the presence of God that can have a genuine impact on how you think, what you think, on your attitudes, words, behavior. I have found that when I am in conflict with someone, realizing that my thoughts are in the presence of God has a way of bringing me to my senses. I can then see more honestly the role I am playing in conflicts I am in and the role I can play in resolving them. That is essential in taking responsibility for your own spiritual development, for distinguishing between thoughts that impede growth and thoughts that lead you to go deeper in your relationship with God and your capacity to love others.

I also recommend music as a way of practicing the presence of God. Music helps us distance ourselves from questions, thoughts, or mental struggles with which we are preoccupied. Most of us think of music as artistic and emotional pleasure. It is both, which is why it can also be therapeutic. Research has found that music supports our mental, physical, emotional, and I would add, spiritual health and well-being. Scientists are finding that music even stimulates memory in the mind of adults suffering from dementia. As one psychologist put it: "Music has the ability to bring us joy and comfort, to motivate us and to help us relax. It has the power to transport us back in time, to calm our worried minds or boost our moods. There really is a song for every emotion."[73]

While religion and great music have a long history together, what with some of the world's greatest composers being church musicians, the power of music for personal spiritual growth is often underused because few people think about it in this way. As a person who is locked into rationalism and for whom logic shapes the way I respond to the world, I have found music to be an avenue into experiencing the depths of spiritual awareness I cannot reach through sheer rationalism. It is tempting to associate religious emotionalism with music because it has been used in this way to manipulate people, especially in worship settings, but that does not diminish the power of music to help us grow spiritually when used responsibly.

Music also builds community because it has the power to connect us with one another in unconscious ways. Neurons in the brain fire with the beat of the music in similar ways among different people which creates an emotional connection between them. Dr. Dacher Keltner, a University of California, Berkeley, psychologist, says, "With music, we feel we're part of community and that has a direct effect on health and well-being."[74] It can even produce a sense of awe, according to David Levitin, a neuroscientist at McGill University, "Music does evoke a sense of wonder and awe for lots of people," something he discovered when he scanned the brains of people while they listened to music.[75]

Perhaps that is why it nurtures us spiritually. I have experienced what I call holy moments in which I have this sudden awareness of what truly matters most in life. It's as if through music I enter into moments when spirit speaks to spirit, and while I often do not have words to describe what I have experienced, because I believe in God I also believe in those moments I am standing on holy ground. What is more, I have found that different kinds of music evoke this kind of experience, from Secret Garden's "A Hymn of Peace" to Puccini's "Nessun dorma." Awe, wonder, inspiration, all qualities that stir an awareness of the divine in life that infuses me with joy and hope. Music, I have discovered, is a gift of God to connect us with the ground of our being which in turn connects us with one another, both of which are the goal of spiritual disciplines.

The final suggestion I have for practicing the presence of God is likely to be the one you find most demanding—offering service to others. When Jesus told his disciples that he "came not to be served but to serve" (Mark 10:45), he was calling them to do the same thing. Why? Because it is the way of love, an expression of spiritual maturity, and, I have found, the way I have experienced the presence of God more than any other way. Serving at a soup kitchen, a shelter for the homeless, or serving food at a homeless encampment in the inner city, have been moments when I am confident that if I did not already believe in God, I would after such an experience. Service ministries may not change the world directly. They may actually be putting a band-aid on an open wound, but they can also change you as you seek to serve rather than to be served, and that changes the world.

I even give money to people when I'm stopped at a street corner or walking by them on the sidewalk. It is possible they throw it away on alcohol or drugs. It's also possible they buy food, as I saw one do recently after I gave him five dollars outside a Quick Trip. The only thing I know for sure is that they are in need or they wouldn't be on the street. Why they are is not my focus. They got there for many different reasons, but the point is, they are there. I never miss the money I give them, and I will never know if it actually helps them. But I can hope that they know someone cares about what happens to them. That enriches my spiritual life whatever it does or doesn't do for them. That is how I experience losing myself on behalf of someone else.

Christian skepticism refuses to let us off the hook when it comes to working out our own salvation in fear and trembling. The freedom it gives for asking questions and challenging established beliefs and norms also takes the Protestant concept of the priesthood of all Christians seriously. You are not dependent on a priest or minister to intercede with God on your behalf. Nurturing your awareness of living life in the presence of God is your way of doing that for yourself. It is the way you put away childish things, childish ways, and accept your status as an adult who takes full responsibility for your relationship to God. It is not an easy thing to do, strange as that may sound. Assuming responsibility for yourself is something all of us say we want as we reach adulthood, but actually doing it has proven itself to be a serious struggle for many people.

Freedom can lead to catastrophe or achievement. In a real sense you have the power to shape the kind of person you become spiritually, but it offers no excuses when you don't, when you grow spiritually stagnant. "We may be born again," the great preacher, Fred Craddock once said, "but we're not born full grown." We have to grow up. That is what we say we want to do when we choose to become a Christian skeptic. We are refusing to let the church, or anyone else, do it for us. We have chosen to work out our own salvation, to own wholeness, if you will, for ourselves. Not to become a better Christian, but to become a better person. That is what being Christian means, and it is enough to make the world a better place for everyone.

13

THE END OF OUR DAYS

The end of anyone's life is hard for somebody, anybody, everybody. Death comes at any time, often out of season, and when it does it turns people's world upside down. The day we are born we begin moving toward its end. We usually don't think about it that way until a death happens that makes us feel vulnerable to unforeseen and uncontrollable forces of life. It is then that death moves from being a concept to it being a reality that is forcing us to live differently because our lives have permanently changed. Suddenly life is different.

Most of the time pastors and churches provide the level of support and comfort people need at what is often the worst moment of their lives. They can also be careless in what is said about death that unintentionally shows insensitivity to the pain, sadness, sense of loss, and fear of the future people are feeling. I have heard pastors speak beautiful words to families in grief and I have also heard them say things that made me want to scream, "Stop! You're not helping." I wish they would say nothing at all, which is exactly what is sometimes needed most. I remember the story about a young rabbinical student accompanying the great Rabbi Abraham Joshua Heschel when he went to a grieving family in observance of Shiva, the seven days of mourning beginning after a funeral. He went in and sat in silence for an hour, then left. The young student didn't understand and asked Rabbi Heschel why he didn't say any of the things appropriate for Shiva. The great man replied, "I didn't need to say anything. They knew I was there."[76]

Rabbi Sari Laufer explains Heschel's actions further when she describes what he taught all his students:

> Rabbi Abraham Joshua Heschel teaches that there are three modes of mourning: silence, tears and song. The rules and traditions of Jewish mourning tell us that we—the comforters—do not get to set the mode and the tone. Grief ebbs and it flows. It can be melancholic and profound, it can be raucous and inappropriate, but whatever it is, it belongs to the mourner. It is the bereaved who can tell you if and what he needs to share, or when she wants to cry or laugh. If the mourner is too stunned to even form a coherent sentence, that's okay, too. Your job, our job, is to be with them where they need to be. Not to coax, not to lead—just to be there.[77]

Perhaps being at a loss for words when people lose a loved one is a good thing. At the very least words spoken should be carefully chosen because the one thing that should never be forgotten or minimized is that a death is death. We may hope it becomes a doorway to what is next, but it is first the end of a relationship, which is the most important part of life. Death is real, often tragic, always the source of pain, and forces on people an abrupt and unwanted necessity for life being permanently changed.

Death reminds us of how unpredictable life is. My father died when he was 63 years old of heart problems. My mother lived to be a hundred. The Yin and Yang of life expectancy. One died too soon, the other when she was at peace with her length of days, grateful for the life she had had and was ready for it to come to an end. "I am not afraid of dying," were among her last words. Yet, looking back a couple of years after she died here in our home, her life seems far too short. My dad's was completely out of season. He should have had more time. I didn't realize how young he truly was until I was a year older than when he died. Perspectives change with aging.

You may be young and thinking about death is the last thing you want to do. But it is a fact of life that is as natural as breathing. No one knows its timing, but that is what makes thinking about death so important. It can and does happen any time and can turn your world upside-down instantly. A middle-age woman can undergo a routine mammogram that detects a dark spot and in a matter of days she is told she has breast cancer. A young adult male has a day when a headache becomes so unbearable his wife takes him to the ER where after a series of tests is told he has a mass on his brain. Both of them know they will not live forever, as do their families, but why at this point in life? Timing is everything.

Because it is, recognizing the brevity of life becomes a sign of wisdom. Scripture refers to life as a vapor: "You do not know what will happen tomorrow. For what is your life? It is even a vapor that appears for a little time and then vanishes away." (James 4:14) I like the way Eugene Peterson paraphrased this text in "The Message":

> And now I have a word for you who brashly announce, "Today—at the latest, tomorrow—we're off to such and such a city for the year. We're going to start a business and make a lot of money." You don't know the first thing about tomorrow. You're nothing but a wisp of fog, catching a brief bit of sun before disappearing. Instead, make it a habit to say, "If the Master wills it and we're still alive, we'll do this or that.

That's the way life seems when you're looking back rather than forward, like an evaporating fog. Everyone who lives long enough to look back knows they have lived longer than they will. You wonder where time has gone. Only yesterday you had your whole life in front of you and now most of it is in the rearview mirror.

There's nothing depressing about it. It's simply the way life works. More than that, one of the ironies of life is that confronting the brevity of life highlights just how precious life is. It's the treasure among treasures, the thing that matters more than anything else. We call it relationships, but relationships are expressions of the gift of life. Being alive is an amazing reality that is easily taken for granted. Rising every morning can be cause for thanksgiving because of the potential the day holds for relationships to be enjoyed, work to be done, discoveries to be made, moments of reflection on what matters most in life being experienced. I often wonder if people whose bodies are broken think about people taking for granted the simple ability to get out of bed without assistance and move through the day on your own, not giving a thought to what a gift just being physically able to meet the day truly is. The older you get, the less you take good health for granted, which means the less you take life for granted.

If you think about it, is there anything more miraculous than life itself? Our first grandson was born prematurely and weighted less than five pounds. Today he is over six feet tall and a wonderful athlete. How did that happen? Most of us don't pay any attention to the process of growing, but it is a stunning reality and you are an amazing reality simply because you are alive. Even if you live with a handicap, or must contend with an illness or disease, you are an amazing reality because you are a person. Life is difficult, but it is also beautiful. Life is short, but its worth is not measured by time but contribution. What you give determines what you get from it. That's why St. Francis of Assisi who gave his life helping the poor ended his inspiring prayer with the words: "for it is in giving that we receive, it is in pardoning that we are pardoned, and it is in dying that we are born to Eternal Life."

What life teaches you is that the fear of dying is a hindrance to living life fully because it focuses your attention on something over which you have no control rather than on what you do control. Life is more than what you make of it because there are many variables outside of your own reach, but your life is largely shaped, formed, and given quality by you. It's called making the most of what you have, and, if you are fortunate, what you have is a life to live of your own choosing. As you age, you begin to look back to see what you've done with it. It is then that you are tempted to have regrets over things said or done or opportunities missed.

Behavioral psychologist Daniel Pink who wrote a book

entitled, The Power of Regret: How Looking Back Moves Us Forward defines "regret" as "a negative emotion in that it's an emotion that makes us feel worse, not better. And it's an emotion that's triggered when we think of something from our past and wish we had done something differently, done something in a different way, not done something, taken an action, not taken an action."[78] He says that more than 80% of adults look back and wish they had done something different from what they did. At the same time, he adds, the older you get, the more regrets are focused on inaction, something you didn't do. Pink also found that people want to talk about regrets, which surprised him. He described it as being like a damn bursting for people when they began to talk about regrets. What he has observed is that when understood as natural, normal, and not a judgment, regrets move us forward because we have the capacity to learn from them. More than that, time allows us to gain perspective not simply on what happened in the past, but on ourselves, on our own growth and development, in the here and now.

That is critical to coping with the fact that not dying means coping with the aging process that can be as difficult as it is inevitable. The closer you get to death, the more you want to live as fully as possible the days you have left. Sadly, American society is not helpful to aging because most Americans tend to equate getting older with becoming useless. Some older people fulfill that expectation, but others don't. The key is the realization that learning has no age limit. I have a friend who in her seventies began taking cello lessons in a class of kids younger than her grandchildren and is now playing regularly in an instrumental quartet. I began studying German seriously with the goal of becoming proficient in it when I retired. Living the life you have is not only for the young. It is for everyone who has breath left in them.

Some of our most important break-throughs happen only because of living a while. One of the examples of that is a man named Atz Kilcher. He is the father of four children, including the world-famous pop singer/song writer, Jewell. The multiple season Discovery Channel T.V. Show, "Alaska: The Last Frontier," has made the Kilcher family public figures. Yule Kilcher and his wife, Ruth, immigrated from Switzerland in the 1940s and established what they called the Homestead in Kachemak Bay, Alaska near the town of Homer. It was a rugged life then, and remains so today. Yule and Ruth raised eight children, including Atz, his younger brother, Otto, who is in the series, and six sisters. Atz came home from the Vietnam War suffering from PTSD. He used alcohol to deal with his emotional pain, both of which made him an abusive father to his children. A single father to four children, three boys and Jewell, his one daughter, after his wife left him, life was such that Jewell finally left home at the age of fifteen. In a People Magazine interview she described it this way: "My dad and I had a difficult relationship, and I thought, 'I could live in a cabin by myself or I could live in a cabin with a guy that isn't that nice to me. So, why not go live in a cabin by myself?"[79]

She did, of course, becoming a major recording artist selling millions of albums and being a multiple Grammy nominee. After several years Jewell finally returned to the Homestead to introduce her own five-year son to his grandfather Atz and her brothers. She encountered a different Atz Kilcher than the one she had known as a girl growing up in a harsh and primitive environment, a man who had mellowed, learned a lot about himself. In one episode she described her father as a man still growing, changing, choosing to be a different person than he had once been. "He got sober," she said in that same People Magazine interview, "and did this amazing inner work. It's a profound transformation. We have a really authentic, great relationship now, but it's because he did his work, and I did my work."

Jewell also says she learned in nature that hard wood grows slow and chose to make it a metaphor for her own life. That is why she and her father have moved past the worst years in their relationship to better ones now. The lesson in their story is that as long as we are alive there is living to do, experiences to have, changes to be made, regrets to be a catalyst for redeeming the past. One of the themes in this book is that human beings are flawed. We make mistakes. We cause trouble, hurt others, hurt ourselves, say and do things we shouldn't say and do. It is not the whole story either, just part of it. Which means it is easy for you to beat up on yourself in looking back over your life as if you should have been better than you were. Perhaps you should have, but the same can be said of everyone else simply because that is part of being human.

But know this. Any reluctance you have in forgiving yourself for past mistakes can make being human worse than it has to be. Genuine forgiveness is not easy anytime, but many, if not most, people find it easier to forgive someone else than to forgive themselves. What that suggests is that you may be tempted to hold yourself to a higher standard than you do others. But remember that forgiveness ultimately begins and ends with God, and the message Jesus gave was that God's forgiveness is "seventy times seven," which means "endless." If you are worth divine forgiveness, you are worth your own.

You may already know this if you have lived a while, or you will sometime in the future, but life is too short to allow regrets, troubles, problems, or anything else to limit your living. As strange as it may sound, especially if you have more years to live than you have lived already, it is in accepting the fact that you will die that frees you to live fully. Of course, no one knows when death will come, and even if you know it comes to everyone, it may well feel untimely simply because you have more living you want to do. The death of a former colleague was a touching reminder of experiencing death that way.

Much more than being an academic, Bill was a genuine scholar with a contemplative spirit that led him periodically to spend time with a community of monks in a nearby monastery even in his retirement years. There his spirit was deepened and renewed, and perhaps was the reason his mind and energy had not been slowed by aging. A couple of weeks before the end came he had led the final session of a weekly class he had convened at his church to study the life of the American Trappist monk, Thomas Merton. He had also taught himself Latin and was engaged daily in the hard work of translating the Gospel of Mark from Latin into English. His stated goal was to be able to read Mark in his Latin Bible without having to look up any words.

He didn't get to finish. At his memorial service one of his daughters recounted a conversation her mother told her she had

had with her father just before he died that captured how he felt about that. Bill's wife, Sally, knew he loved the Psalms, reading and praying them daily. The title of one of his books was, Taste and See, taken from Psalm 34:8: "Taste and see that the Lord is good." It was only natural that she asked him if he would like for her to read him a Psalm. He told her no, adding, "There is no Psalm angry enough for how I am right now."

I have thought many times since hearing that story that what Bill said was a remarkable affirmation of the gift life truly is. In his candor characteristic of the Psalms themselves, he was expressing anger about dying because he savored every minute of time life afforded him to explore, question, and research the richness of the Christian tradition, to teach what he had learned, to be an active participant in the church he loved, and to enjoy the gift of a family he dearly loved. Death was not something he feared. It was something that made him angry for cutting short his life story before he had time to finish writing it.

I can't think of a better way to go out, mad at death for cutting short the time you have to explore the gift life truly is, to go as deep as possible into its mystery, to give and receive love, and to indeed taste and see that the Lord is good. His words at the end reminded me of the Dylan Thomas poem, "Do Not Go Gentle Into the Good Night" that begins with the lines:

> Do not go gentle into that good night,
> Old age should burn and rave at close of day;
> Rage, rage against the dying of the light.

That's what Bill did in his own quiet way, rage, rage, against the dying of the light, and in doing so bore testimony to the gift life is. The most basic truth in life is that our days will end sometime. Using that as a motivator for living your life fully is similar to being honest about your regrets. Naming them disarms their power to cause fear or dread. After all, your life started moving toward its end the moment you were born. But what you are doing with it in-between the two is what matters, in fact, all that matters.

But one question still remains. What impact does believing in the resurrection of Jesus have on the end of our days? It is a question only for Christians, but whose answer may offer good news beyond Christianity. My answer begins with believing that Jesus was bodily raised from the dead. It may surprise you that I say that, even strike you as antiscientific and a contradiction to my commitment to being a Christian skeptic. I have friends who have said that to me, suggesting that I am being irrational. My response is that if I believe in God, then it makes perfectly good sense to believe in the resurrection. That's because, contrary to what many Christians believe, the resurrection is not about Jesus. Nor is it any kind of "proof" that Jesus was divine. In point of fact, the divinity of Jesus has no bearing on his resurrection. It's not about him at all. It is about God.

This is crucial to understand. Believing in the resurrection of Jesus because you believe he was divine, or the reverse, that the resurrection is proof that he was divine, not only misses the point, but distracts from it. Believing in the resurrection is a statement of faith in God, not Jesus. Believing in God means that you believe God is the Creator of life in the first place, thus, it is a natural and easy step to believe that God can bring life out of death. It's all about whether or not you believe in God.

This is how believing in God is a life-changing choice. Once you choose to believe God is real, that necessarily means you cannot place limits on God lest by doing so you are de facto saying you do not actually believe in God. A God subject to limitations assigned by human beings is the creation of the human mind. By definition, if God exists, then God is sovereign. Thus, limitations placed on God are self-contradictory. If life comes from God in the first place, it is logical to say that God is capable of breathing life again into what dies.

But believing in the resurrection of Jesus not only affirms belief in God, it also affirms your belief in life after death. It is possible to believe in life after death without believing in the resurrection. It is not possible, on the other hand, to believe in the resurrection and not believe in life after death. The resurrection of Jesus is in fact the Christian affirmation of life after death. And, to push the argument further, believing in the resurrection which is an affirmation of believing in life after death in turn becomes a statement of faith in the reality of God. In short, God, the resurrection of Jesus, life after death, are three statements of faith that go together like a hand in glove. They make sense together more than they do separately.

People who don't believe in God naturally believe life ends at death. My former colleague quoted in the chapter on religion and science puts it this way:

> I believe that after I die, my consciousness will cease to exist, and from my standpoint will be as it was in 1948, before I existed. The difference is that there will be people who will remember me, will presumably miss me, who I hope will think the world has been made a little better by my having been in it. I consider consciousness, this mysterious self-awareness in a marvelous universe that is full of wonder and wonderful things, and populated by fellow conscious beings, to be an incredible gift. To be granted, if you are lucky, seven or eight decades of this and then to ask for more? That just seems greedy to me.

And then he adds this:

> I have no evidence that would mean anything to a scientist to support my position. It is opinion only, even if it is opinion based on at least two sides of that Wesleyan quadrilateral. But then, neither does anyone else have that sort of evidence for their position. So I'm not going to yell at anybody. I'm not going to pity anybody and think they are simple minded. I judge people by what they do. If they do good, then they are good people. People are motivated to do good for all sorts of reasons. I care a lot more about the deeds than the motivations.

What he says makes sense to anyone who has reached the conclusion he has that God does not exist. He respects people who believe in God, but is unable to go there himself. That he is a very good man is, of course, what truly matters. But what he says at the end needs to be highlighted. He admits that his rejection of the reality of God is an opinion, not a statement of fact. In other words, he affirms that when it comes to believing or not believing in God, both views have reason and logic behind them, but at the end of the day neither is a fact, only a belief.

So as a Christian skeptic, I believe in God, the resurrection of Jesus, and life after death. Each impacts my life, but together they do something else whose importance transcends everything else. They give me hope to live now. And while the Apostle Paul said that among faith, hope, and love, love is the greatest of all, I have found that having hope gets me up in the morning and keeps me going so I can continue to believe love is more powerful than hate, and good is more powerful than evil. In the next chapter I explain why.

†

14

CHRISTIAN SKEPTICISM AND HOPE

At first glance, skepticism seems to be antithetical to hope, always asking questions and never being satisfied until it has some answers. Hope, on the other hand, is an attitude that exists when the answers are discouraging or non-existent. In real life, though, skepticism can clear the way for hope by exposing false hope that pretends things are better than they are or rests on unrealistic expectations. Because hope does not live in a vacuum, but arises from actual circumstances, it must cope with what is before it can think about what might be in the future. Skepticism helps people sort through the "what is" honestly and carefully in order to help people not jump to conclusions based on worries and fears instead of actual circumstances.

Let me share a story to put what I am saying in a real-life situation.

Dr. Paul E. Johnson, one of the major pioneers in the field of pastoral care and counseling was teaching a graduate class I was taking that included the use of what was called "verbatims" which were as close as possible a word for word account of a pastoral situation each class member had to submit for class evaluation. One of them I remember was a verbatim from a student who described a conversation he had with a woman in the hospital who had cancer. As he was leaving, she asked him to pray for her healing. The verbatim was honest about the struggle he had with her request. Neither of them knew what her future was going to be, but praying for someone's healing was not anything he had ever done before, and he admitted that he didn't believe that was how prayer worked. In the end he said he prayed for her comfort and strength to face whatever she faced in the days ahead, but he didn't pray for God to heal her.

Our responses to his verbatim were characteristically supportive, expressing understanding about the difficult situation he was in, even sympathy for the awkward position in which her request had put him. Dr. Johnson listened attentively until we had exhausted our evaluations of how he handled the situation and then asked the presenter a single question, "Why did you give up to the doctors?"

The room went quiet. The question gave all of us pause. I remember wondering if Dr. Johnson was suggesting praying for the woman might actually heal her, or that the student should have given her reason to believe it would. In the discussion that followed it became clear that he was challenging the belief that the prognosis for the woman should be the final and only word for her in the circumstances she was facing. Dr. Johnson pointed out that her request in itself was her way of saying she was struggling to find a reason to live the days she had left when the doctor had taken away all hope for the future. That was not the intention of her doctor, but it was clearly the effect. He was simply being honest to avoid giving her false hope, the same desire the student had, which is why Dr. Johnson asked him why he gave up to the doctor.

It was a question a skeptical mind asks. A medical diagnosis is the best conclusion a doctor can reach based on the evidence available, but hope is never based solely on evidence. It doesn't deny the facts, only that things happen beyond what is known, things that fall into the category, dare we say, of "mystery." Who has not heard stories of a "miracle" healing, which to the skeptical mind is a way of describing an event no one predicted would take place based on what was known at the time. A skeptic might resist the reason given for the "miracle," such as God intervened, but it doesn't deny that something unusual happened that still has no explanation.

Looking back all these years later, I think Dr. Johnson was suggesting to all of us in the class that people look to ministers to be messengers of hope precisely because we represent God to them which in turn reminds them that there is more to circumstances than what the facts may be saying. Skepticism rejects both the certainty with which some people speak of God's intervention in a situation and the certainty that what will happen in the future is determined solely by known facts. Dr. Johnson realized the student was in a very difficult situation and responded with pastoral concern and integrity, but also reminded all of us that faith involves confronting the mystery built into the fabric of life.

The entire foundation for faith in God is the acceptance of the truth that while we humans know a lot, we don't know everything. Life is mystery as much as God is. Believing in God is the way we trust that there is more to reality than what we see, touch, feel, think, or experience. Practically, this means faith opens the door to hope regardless of circumstances because our faith enables us to trust that God is the final word. The reason for being Christian is not to be or to do good. You can do both without being Christian. The reason for being Christian is not to make the world better. Again, you can do that without being Christian. The reason for being Christian is not to get to heaven. If heaven were a place (which it isn't, as I have previously said), that would be self-serving, which would be a contradiction to what being Christian means. Instead of any of these, being Christian is about not losing hope.

It is possible for people who don't believe in God to have hope in difficult circumstances, but it is equally true that anyone who believes in God always has reason to hope whatever the circumstances are. To lose hope is to give up on life, the consequences of which can be severe enough to cause death. Victor Frankl wrote about this kind of power hope has in people's lives in his book, Man's Search For Meaning.[80] Men who survived the three camps he was in never lost hope, he said, while many of those who lost hope did not survive. The horror of the Holocaust was, of course, unique, but the power of hope is redemptive in all situations. The unexpected dimension to being a person who doesn't give up on hope is that hope strengthens hope. Just as cynicism begets cynicism, negativity begets negativity, so, too, positivity begets positivity, love begets love, and hope begets hope.

In his book, The Dignity of Difference by Rabbi Jonathan Sacks, a world-renown British thinker and philosopher, wrote, "Optimism is the belief that things will get better. Hope is the faith that, together, we can make things better. Optimism is a passive virtue; hope is an active one. It takes no courage to be an optimist, but it takes a great deal of courage to have hope."[81]

Hope is more substantive than optimism because the latter depends on the circumstances in a situation getting better. Hope doesn't because it is not based on circumstances. That is not a small thing. In difficult circumstances, external factors seldom offer much reason for hope. Indeed, they become reasons to lose hope, to give up and accept bad circumstances as determinative of everything that will follow. But hope doesn't look to external factors for support or encouragement. It looks beyond them to values grounded in trust that God is present whatever the circumstances, that God is working through relationships to help you get through what you're facing. Hope enables you to hold on to your faith in a caring God who knows you, loves you, and in turn that emboldens hope. It takes the long view and looks to what lies ahead as well as what is right in front of us. Hope is realistic instead of optimistic. Being hopeful doesn't mean you see things through a rose-colored lens. It means you see things exactly the way they are, but you also see beyond those things. This is why it strikes me as very strange to think that a person who believes in God would not be hopeful. It is in the very nature of faith in God to place trust in truth and goodness and love to ultimately prevail over falsehood, evil, and hate. To give up hope is to miss the core meaning of faith. It is the equivalent of being a mountain climber, but never experiencing the ultimate quest of reaching the summit.

I realize that such talk can sound pious and unreal, but the testimony of Christians throughout history says it is far more than that. Dr. Eberhard Bethge,[82] the brother-in-law of Dietrich Bonhoeffer and someone with whom I had the personal privilege of getting to know when he spent a semester-in-residence at the college where I was chaplain, on more than one occasion recounted the story of Bonhoeffer being led to the gallows where he was to be hanged saying to a fellow prisoner as he passed him, "This is the end—but for me, the beginning." Only a man with hope could say that. Because he was Christian, Bonhoeffer trusted himself to a loving God and that gave him the strength he needed to face his own unjust death.

I think the Apostle Paul was saying something similar when he wrote, "We know that all things work together for good for those who love God, who are called according to his purpose." (Romans 8:28) Eugene Peterson's paraphrase of this verse in The Message reads, "That's why we can be so sure that every detail in our lives of love for God is worked into something good." Paul underscored the same theme in a different way when he wrote: "For I am convinced that neither death, nor life, nor angels, nor rulers, nor things present, nor things to come, nor powers, nor height, nor depth, nor anything else in all creation will be able to separate us from the love of God in Christ Jesus our Lord." (Romans 8:38-39)

Believing in God makes believing that God is the end of all things and we, therefore, have nothing to fear. A Christian skeptic can affirm both that kind of trust and the worthwhileness of life that make every day a gift for which to be grateful. At the same time, a skeptical mind doesn't shy away from the reality of evil that makes believing in God difficult and not losing hope in the worst of circumstances. No one has to convince a Christian skeptic that evil is real. Acts of evil are everywhere. Vladimir Putin targeting civilians in his war against Ukraine killing children, mothers, fathers is an act of evil. The Hamas attack in 2023 on Israeli civilians that killed 1,139, injured many others, and resulted in hostages being taken was an act of evil. Israeli bombing of Palestinian civilians in Gaza in response to the Hamas attack was an evil act. Slavery was evil. Segregation was evil. Apartheid was evil. The local teenage son who shot his brother, his father, and beat his mother to death with a hammer was an evil act. Evil is everywhere and anywhere.

How and why are questions with no simple answers. Is a socio-path who has no sense of right or wrong an evil person? Was Hitler an evil man or was the evil in what he did, or both?

What about those who supported him or did what he ordered? Were they evil, or just what they did? In a sense, it doesn't matter because evil is real whether we understand it or not. Bad things happen to good people, bad people, all people. It's called life, and sometimes those bad things can take the life out of you. That is when hope becomes the most important quality you can possess, hope despite circumstances. Hope insists that evil never has the last word. God does.

People can debate whether or not someone can live without hope, but the more important question is why anyone would want to. Hope is a choice you have to make just as believing in God is. Anyone who has made the choice to trust in God naturally chooses to hope. Hope exists because it is the inevitable fruit born of faith that there is a good God who created life and will not let it die. It is tempting to exaggerate the impact hope can have in your life. The prophet Isaiah declared:

> But those who wait for the LORD shall renew their strength,
> they shall mount up with wings like eagles,
> they shall run and not be weary, they shall walk and not faint.

I cannot say that holding on to hope has ever made me feel like I could soar like an eagle or run and never get weary or walk and never grow faint. But I can say that hope is why I refuse to give up on life having meaning and purpose and continue to believe that my life and yours matter, that joy is real, that love connects us to the greatest mystery of all, and that we are connected to one another because we all belong to God.

15

THE WAY FORWARD

On October 1, 2024 Jimmy Carter became the first former President of the United States to turn one hundred years of age. But I think the former president will be remembered less for his presidency than for his humanity. Soon after leaving office, he and Rosalynn, his beloved wife of seventy-seven years who died in 2023, founded the Carter Work Project, in cooperation with Habitat for Humanity, whose purpose since its founding has been to bring thousands of volunteers together to build affordable housing across the world, thus far, in fourteen countries. In addition, they founded the Carter Center, a nonprofit promoting democracy and global development. In 2002, the former President received the Nobel Peace Prize for his efforts to find solutions to international conflicts, and his work on behalf of human rights that was a hallmark of his four years in the White House.

Jimmy Carter lived the life he lived because, as he would have said, he was being Christian. His life was what living Christian in today's world looks like. We don't know what he believed about the things we have discussed in this book, but we do know that he withdrew from the Southern Baptist Convention to which his family had belonged for generations because it insisted that the Bible says women should be subservient to men. Not only do we not know what his personal beliefs were in regard to the things Southern Baptists are supposed to believe, we would be no better off if we did. All we need to know to be inspired by his life (and Rosalynn's) is to look at how he lived.

That is the way it should be, but we know it isn't, and in broad terms we know why. Christianity grew out of the Jesus movement of the 1st century. Once it became organized it became the church, the ecclesia, "the called out." Christians, then, were a group of people who separated themselves from the world by choosing to live by the example Jesus set and the teachings he gave for how to live a life devoted to God. But through the centuries the church has grown closer to the world and farther from the message of Jesus. That is how the distinction between being Christian and being a Christian transitioned from a distinction without a difference to a difference that is real. The argument I have been making is that the key to that difference is that the church turned Christianity into what you believe rather than keeping the focus on how you live.

I believe this is why the most pressing issue facing Christianity today is the same one Bonhoeffer said his church was facing, how to live the Christian life in the modern world. Countless individual Christians have learned on their own how to do that. They should have learned it in church, or at least been able to stay in the church once they did. Focusing on right beliefs makes it easy to forget that values grounded in the teachings of Jesus matter more than anything else. Christianity has been a blessing in and to the world when faith has been incarnated in people faithful to the values Jesus lived and taught. Nothing good ever comes from a Christianity that lets minor things become major and major things slip into the background. For Christians, putting first things first means following the man Jesus in order to live as he did and, thus, as we can.

At the end of the day, though, the problems Christians have created for ourselves is not simply the content of the beliefs, though that can be a problem, too. It is, instead. how we have treated the things we believe, often worshipping them instead of God which inevitably leads to excluding instead of including anyone and everyone who wants to be included. Given what scientists now know about the human brain, the church's insistence that its teachings about God, Jesus, the Bible, science, the world, non-Christians, and everything else is of divine origin is how it justifies the elevation of and forced conformity to its beliefs. But the human brain, as science shows us, does not function like a camcorder or camera.[83] Neuroscientist Pascal Wallisch puts it this way, the eye is not a video camera and the brain does not just passively record its input."[84] It functions more like an artist painting a picture, processing information that creates ideas and thoughts and views and opinions based on the images coming to life at the hand of the artist. Nothing is ever the way we see it, remember it, or what we believe about it. More than that, our brains never stop processing information, which means our perceptions are in a state of constant flux.

Healthy brains don't function in some people and not in others. Healthy brains function in similar ways in everyone. The quality of the function may differ, and which part of the brain is functioning may not be the same at a given moment for everyone, but everyone's brain functions like everyone else's, Christians included. It makes Christianity less believable when the church (or individual Christians) refuses to acknowledge that religious beliefs are formed through normal brain functions. Everything the church has ever said or will say about anything and everything, including God and Jesus, is the result of the way we humans process information. We cannot think about God except by using the brain we were born with. When people come together they can collectively think better, imagine better, and create better than one brain can alone, but that collective by-product is still limited by the fact that it is the result of natural human brain processes.

The way forward for Christianity and the American church is to embrace skepticism precisely because everything Christians believe is the result of the way the brain works. As wise, insightful, profound, and true any church teaching may be, all of it is the result of human thought. Nothing Christianity says is from God. It is only and always has been and always will be what we believe came from God, believe is the will of God, trust how God wants us to think and to act. Authority for any belief is an internal human process of confirmation and affirmation. The church of the future will need to recognize that its authority or that of the Bible cannot be imposed because that is not how the brain works. Power can be maintained externally, but acceptance of authority demands more than coercion or a show of force. If it doesn't make sense or correspond with what people already know or contradicts personal experience, for most people it will have no authority.

Today more than ever people bring their brains with them when they enter the church door and immediately begin to process what they see and hear. The same thing happens when they hear someone making claims about what the Bible says. Some people condition themselves to accept what they are told and shut down thoughts that contradict it. But Christian skeptics are equipped to recognize that fallacy before falling into it because we are constantly engaged in critically evaluating what we see, hear, or read. That is why being skeptical involves hard work, but work that has its own reward. It helps to take us out of ourselves and refocuses our attention on the needs of others because we don't have anything to protect. Because of what Jesus said and did in his own life, we know our task is to "go do likewise," to love our neighbors the way we love ourselves which leads us into such actions as compassion, forgiveness, justice, respect for others, to name a few. We may struggle to live by these values, but we know that we are supposed to.

Being a Christian skeptic also eliminates the fear that truth will destroy faith. When your focus is on living your life as authentically as Jesus lived his, fears born of the pursuit of right beliefs disappear. As demanding as being Christian is, it allows space to think freely which in and of itself brings a sense of joy at being alive. Thinking is hard work, but entertaining great ideas and wrestling with critical issues adds to life's meaning and purpose.

Answers used to interest me when I was younger, but they don't anymore, not least because I have finally accepted the fact that I don't have many, and none when it comes to the most perplexing issues we face today. Questions are the stuff of life, and, as one of my academic colleagues would often remind us, every issue has at least two sides. That is why there are no easy answers except pseudo-ones. A skeptical mind doesn't mind hard questions. That is precisely why theology is so fascinating.

As a friend reminded me, it's all about the joy of the "holy interrogatory."

Living Christian in today's world as a skeptic provides a credible reason for others to see that having all the answers or even some of them is not what being Christian means. Being free and comfortable enough to ask questions is the kind of Christian example American culture needs to see. One of the surest things in life is that people who claim to have the answers don't. At the opposite end of the spectrum, people who admit they don't are being intellectually honest. Questions always outnumber answers when it comes to faith, which is why the quest for certainty reflects a misunderstanding of the nature of faith. Being a skeptic encourages us to constantly stretch the limits of Christian beliefs without fear because we know that at the end of our days we will be remembered, as we now remember former President Jimmy Carter, not for what we believed, but by how well we did at living Christian.

†

POSTSCRIPT FOR MINISTERS
(AND EVERYONE IN MINISTRY)

Even though this book is more about Christianity than the church, the two are inextricably intertwined to the point where the future of one is directly affected by the future of the other. That means church leadership will play a key role in the existence of the church and credibility of Christianity going forward. Moreover, that leadership will be focused primarily at the congregational level. There are other important manifestations of church beyond congregations, but what happens at the congregational level of church life determines what happens at other levels because that is where people are. It was that conviction, in fact, that led me several years ago to give up my tenured seminary faculty position, throw caution to the wind, and at the invitation of our denomination, join my wife, Joy, in starting a new congregation.

    I was ordained to ministry over fifty years ago. At the time, I was not thinking about being a minister, and when the moment came when the thought entered my mind and embedded itself in my heart, I was not happy about it. I later discovered that such is the way of call, a story I have already told earlier in the book. I have a deep sense of gratitude that I am still in ministry, yet, at the same time, I wouldn't wish ministry on anyone. It is a difficult life in so many ways, even as it is rewarding and satisfying. Church members often speak and act in ways that are not Christian by any definition, and also rise to the occasion showing wisdom and courage and a commitment to

God that gives you faith in the goodness of humanity. Ministry that can be dispiriting to the most seasoned minister can also provide opportunities to be present to people at their most vulnerable moments in life. Ministry puts you in the middle of the greatest challenges of a given moment in history simply because everything in life that matters is ultimately connected to why we humans are here in the first place and what we must do to sustain life together.

I am not telling you anything you don't already know. You know that as a minister you are in a position to provide the best guidance you can to people who struggle to live and to find meaning and purpose in their lives. That is a responsibility few people are given, but it goes to the heart of what being a minister involves. Ministry is about leadership with a group of people who need help making their lives count for something beyond mere existence. That takes a special kind of leadership, one which is usually taken for granted and seldom appreciated for the significant role it plays in making the world a better place, but leadership without which our church, Christianity, and the nation will flounder worse than they are at the moment.

Leadership, of course, is everything, regardless of the organization or institution, whether it be a business, school, government, or church. Good leadership doesn't guarantee success for the group, but poor leadership guarantees that whatever goals, mission, or purpose the group has will be more difficult to achieve. For the church, leadership may be the most pressing need it has right now, not because there is a shortage of ministers, though there is. Rather, because, as one of my former colleagues used to say, there is always a shortage of good ministers. Naturally, a variety of factors make for a good minister, but chief among them is the capacity to read the times in order to know what is undermining the church's understanding of what it means to be church.

At the moment, I suspect you already know that Christian Nationalism is having that kind of effect as a false version of what Christianity is. You are also likely to have members who don't realize that or understand why it is so dangerous. I would imagine that preaching is one of the most challenging elements of ministry today because of the political divisions our nation is experiencing that are made worse by Christians who think that what they believe the Bible says should govern America rather than the Constitution. You are called to be the pastor and preacher to all members of your congregation, not just those who understand what Christianity actually is. But how you do that in a way that is faithful to your calling cannot be easy, or even at times, clear.

What may help is to remember that this is not the first time American clergy have faced this kind of challenge. From the early days of our country when the white Europeans who landed on these shores began to treat native Americans as savages, to the inhumanity of the slave trade, to the Civil War, to a segregated South, preachers have had to speak truth to power at great risk. In more recent times many of us have been where you are. I entered ministry and began preaching in student congregations just as the civil rights movement was at its greatest strength under the leadership of Martin Luther King, Jr., and then faced one of its worst moments when he was assassinated.

The civil rights movement was a Civil War of a different kind. When the first one ended the nation was supposed to go beyond black Americans being free from being owned. The nation was supposed to ensure just treatment under the law for black men and women who stood equal to their former white slave owners. Instead, racial segregation became another name for slavery in the South, only more pernicious in hiding the white supremacy that undergirded slavery itself. This is why the second Civil War became necessary, only this time it was a non-violent assault on white supremacy itself in the South. The civil rights movement recognized that indentured racism was no better than outright slavery and, thus, had to be permanently ended.

One of the primary institutions that faced the choice to stand up for racial justice or support racial injustice and segregation was the church. Most, especially in the South, chose the latter, forcing clergy into a crisis of conscience. One of the ministers for whom I worked as a youth minister was dismissed by his church for preaching sermons in support of civil rights. When I became a student pastor a couple of years later I was cursed by a church member for having a moment of silent prayer during morning worship for the Martin Luther King family as President Johnson had asked churches to do the Sunday after he was assassinated. Those were times that demanded faithfulness from clergy over job security. We knew what was right. Doing it was the problem. Even worse was not doing it and living with yourself. Was staying in a church that refused to support racial justice even worth it?

Such circumstances placed enormous demands on clergy to be the kind of leaders ministry demanded and churches needed even when they didn't know they did. I believe you are facing similar circumstances today. How do you preach in ways that speak to all sides in our divided environment with passions running high and reason in short supply? Partisanship openly takes priority over commitment to the gospel of Jesus just as racism did fifty years ago. Russell Moore, editor in chief at the conservative magazine Christianity Today wrote a story about multiple Southern Baptist pastors telling him of being confronted by church members after giving a sermon highlighting the words of Jesus from the Sermon on The Mount with the question, "Where did you get those liberal talking points?" When the minister responded, "I'm literally quoting Jesus Christ," the church member said, "Yes, but that doesn't work anymore. That's weak."[85]

Is it any wonder that so many ministers are quitting, as we noted earlier in the book, or that fewer and fewer are choosing to become one? Why would anyone choose to spend his or her life working under that kind of stress? Yet, without effective leadership churches will lose touch with the costs of discipleship more than they have already. Many of them will be unaware that they have chosen the path of "cheap grace" that demands no cost from them for being Christian. In today's America where greed and materialism are rampant and the desire for more seems insatiable, preaching a message of sacrificing for the sake of others and calling people to choose personal integrity over political party loyalty requires courage and toughness.

In this kind of church environment, honest preaching must feel like you're taking your life into your own hands every week. Yet, the stakes couldn't be higher. It's not only a matter of the survival of the church, but the survival of Christianity itself. While I have no particular wisdom in regard to what such leadership looks like, I do remember some of the things that helped me and others in previous times when congregational ministers faced a similar challenge.

What comes to mind immediately as essential is being your congregation's resident theologian. The primary task of every minister is to do theology. That is your vocation, your calling. Church life today expects clergy to serve in various roles, whether it be pastor, administrator, financial manager, or pastoral counselor, but the one many churches want ministers to push aside is being the community's theologian, to teach and preach theology as the foundation for everything else the minister and church do together. Without theological education done in congregations, they become organizations, a church but not church.

Theology is what the church does because it is called to live for God. Theology is not something to study, it is short-hand for living Christian that happens only when people think about God in their daily lives. That is how God moves from being the proverbial abstract to the concrete in people's lives. Teaching theology is what pastors do. Theology is the work of discerning, understanding, perceiving the will of God in the biblical witness and in history. Without theology, Christianity is another version of humanism, not a bad thing, but unfaithful to its calling.

Theology teaches the value of questions, the need for Christians to be skeptics in order to discern truth, to separate the chaff from the wheat, so to speak, to recognize when beliefs not only substitute for living Christian, but lead to actions that contradict the meaning of it. Clergy need to equip their church members to ask the right questions about the intersection of Christian living and modern life as they connect the dots between the life and teachings of Jesus and issues of every kind and shape they face daily. That, I am convinced, holds the key to churches being vital centers of community that can once again contribute to strengthening the universal values that are necessary for human survival.

That is not likely to happen without a serious theological conversation involving a wholesale rethinking of what it means to be church. You are the key to that conversation taking place. I believe it will take a long time for American Christianity to repair the damage it has done to itself, but the work needs to start now. Theologian Stanley Hauerwas, not known for mincing words, summarized why the challenge is so daunting when he wrote, "Protestant Christians set out to make America Christian and ended up making Christianity American."[86]

Leadership in the church now that such a reversal has happened makes the task of clergy engaging the church in a holy conversation about what it means to be Christian and to be the church all the more urgent. Church members must learn to think about God in all the circumstances of their lives, to think in the presence of God, if you will, so that words spoken and decisions made reflect a choice to trust in God as the final reality in their lives. What is more, you will find that the more theology you do, the more grounded you will become in your call to ministry.

Ultimately call is what led you to be in ministry, and call will always be the final arbiter of whether or not you stay. Call falls into the realm of mystery because it arises from the trust that God is real. Ministry exists only for those people who believe they have been called by God to a specific form of service. If God has placed a call on your life, and as much as it will be a struggle to remain faithful to it, in the end you will know that it is the animating purpose of your life. Discouragement is real, but it always has been. The week after I was cursed that Sunday after Martin Luther King, Jr. was assassinated, I was ready to quit ministry and the church. I spent days agonizing over how to resign graciously. As I was searching for a biblical text to use, I came upon the following passage: "Therefore, having this ministry by the mercy of God, we do not lose heart...we have this treasure in earthen vessels, to show that the transcendent power belongs to God and not to us. We are afflicted in every way, but not crushed; perplexed, but not driven to despair; persecuted, but not forsaken; struck down, but not destroyed" (2 Corinthians 4:1, 4-9)

It was not what I wanted to hear, but all these years later I still remember that the message I heard in those verses was that I was still called to ministry and quitting was not an option.

I never doubted my call even once after that experience, even though I have experienced difficult times just as you have. I cannot say I never wanted to quit ministry again, but I can say I knew I couldn't. It had claimed me, just as it has claimed you.

I underscore the centrality of call because it is the source of strength and courage needed to be your congregation's resident theologian. The task you face is difficult and risky because the current circumstances have created the need for you to lead your people away from being a church toward being church. That will require a change in values, something people usually resist strongly. Congregations are functioning the way people want them to even when what they are doing cannot and will not build communities of faith whose values challenge American culture. It will take time for you to teach them the difference, time you will not have until you convince your people that much of what they spend their time doing is much ado about nothing.

That may sound harsh, but no less true. Congregations have learned well how to waste time on matters of monumental insignificance, consciously or unconsciously ensuring they don't have time for what counts. Nothing is more spiritually draining than maintenance ministry, having to create things for people to do to make them feel like being in church is worth their time. American congregations have been doing everything from endless committee meetings to forming clubs to building recreational centers to this end. What I am suggesting is that it is time for congregations to stop most of what they are doing in order to make space and time to learn for the first time again what it means to be church.

There has never been a more urgent time for making this choice. The day before the final draft of this book was sent to my publisher, Donald Trump was elected President of the United States for the second time. It was more than the election of the nation's leader, it was a confirmation, and some would say, exacerbation, of the significant divisions among the American people, including the Christian community. Some Christians voted against Trump, believing him to be morally unfit and a threat to democracy because of his affinity for "strong man" autocratic leaders around the world. Other Christians voted for

Trump, believing him to be an instrument of God to save the nation from moral collapse and the kind of autocratic leader our nation needs right now. The issue of immigration is another flash point of division, So, too, are women's healthcare, including abortion rights, and continuing social struggles related to race, gender identity and gay rights.

How do you preach the gospel when the political divide over these issues in the nation runs through most congregations and denominations? Do you speak boldly of the command to love one's neighbor including everyone and excluding no one for any reason? Do you use the Leviticus text that says, "When an alien resides with you in your land, you shall not oppress the alien. The alien who resides with you shall be to you as the citizen among you; you shall love the alien as yourself, for you were aliens in the land of Egypt: I am the Lord your God." (19:33-34) Do you highlight the Torah commandment that says quite unequivocally that to tell lies about your neighbor is wrong? (Exodus 20:16) I ask these questions because, just as the historical context matters when you want to read the Bible honestly, the contemporary context matters when you read the times honestly.

These are the circumstances for ministry you face every day. No one knows what the shape of being church in America will take in the coming years, but what we do know is that good leaders will be as important then and as they are now. That is precisely the kind of challenge that gives ministry purpose. But it will never happen without you. This is the ministry to which you have been called. Don't lose heart. To be called is to be chosen for a holy purpose of guiding people into claiming their heritage as the "bene ha-Elohim," the children of God. That is truly a holy calling, never easy to live up to, but always worthy of everything it asks of you.

ACKNOWLEDGEMENTS

No book comes to life without a little help from its friends. In my case, a lot of friends. I am in debt, significant debt, in fact, to more than a few people who bear no responsibility for the quality of the content of this book, but who were willing to read it at its early stages and offered criticisms and suggestion that have made it far better than it would be. I want to acknowledge them directly.

Thank you, Wilbur Ressler and Charlie Curry, for taking the time to write suggestions for changes and raising question for me to weigh as I was writing. And thank you Pen Curry, Heather Cargill, Rollie and Becky Bible, Heather Allen, Jon and Jan Halleen, Don and Corrine Slaughter, Lynda Zakarisen, Joe and Darla Standal, Dirk Niles, Nancy Haddorf, Jeanne Sarych, Guy and Cindy Linn for being willing to discuss the book over several weeks during our online Sunday morning worship hour, especially Cindy. Thank you for putting in extra time to reading the material, offering comments and questions that proved invaluable in sharpening the clarity of what I was trying to say.

Thank you, Neal Summerlin, for reading the material as the thoughtful and gracious scientist you are, and for being willing to respond with the kind of intellectual integrity and personal honesty everyone who knows you has come to respect, and for permission to share in writing the personal context in which your evaluation of the material was cradled.

Thomas Minton and David Digby, colleagues in ministry, I owe both of you a special debt of gratitude for being willing to bring your depth and breadth of theological knowledge and insight to a critical reading of the material that a book of this nature requires. You went beyond the call of duty in the work you put in and the encouragement you offered. That is the kind of debt that can never be repaid, but I can at least acknowledge it with the promise that it will not soon be forgotten.

Finally, I want to say to you, Joy, that my life is blessed beyond measure because of the life we have together, and my writing is always enriched because you love me enough to read every page numerous times and then tell me the truth about the good, the bad, and the ugly parts. I love you for doing that. Even more, I love you for you.

Finally, my thanks to James Smith and Carl Condit at Sunstone Press whose enthusiasm for the book when I first proposed it to them assured me that my own belief in its value was more than my personal investment in it. It is both a pleasure and a privilege to work with both of you.

NOTES

1. Facebook post, June 18, 2022. Spong was an American Bishop of the Episcopal Church and a prominent advocate for progressive Christianity.
2. "Harrison Butker's Comments on Olympics Opening Ceremony Goes Viral," by Kaitlin Lewis, Night Reporter, Newsweek online (https://www.newsweek.com/harrison-butker-comments-olympics-opening-ceremony-goes-viral. In a commencement address at Benedictine College in Atchison, Kansas in 2024, Butker also urged women graduates to get married, become homemakers, and have babies.
3. Unbinding Christianity: Choosing the Values of Jesus over the Beliefs of the Church (Universal Press, 2020)
4. Dietrich Bonhoeffer, The Cost of Discipleship (NY: Macmillan Paperback Edition, 1963), p. 60.

Chapter 2

5. "How To Be A True Skeptic," https://bigthink.com/hard-science/how-to-be-a-true-skeptic/.
6. Steven Novella, The Skeptics Guide to the Universe: How to Know What's Real in a World Increasingly Full of Fake (NY: Grand Central Publishing, 2018).
7. P.19.
8. P.18.
9. P.54)

10. M. Scott Peck, The Road Less Traveled (Touchstone; Anniversary Edition, March 13, 2012).
11. Novella, p. 5
12. Mark A. Noll, The Civil War as a Theological Crisis (The University of North Carolina Press. Kindle Edition, pp.1-2.
13. This is how Noll describes Philip Schaff who he says was the nation's most versatile religious scholar in the 1860s and wrote an article justifying slavery as "an immense blessing to the whole race of Ham." Schaff was, Noll says, a "representative of his age" (p.51).
14. (https://www.inf.fu-berlin.de/lehre/pmo/eng/Dawkins-MindViruses.pdf).
15. The Selfish Gene (Oxford University Press; 2nd edition, October 25, 1990).
16. https://cdlib.org/cdlinfo/2018/01/12/reports-of-ezids-death-are-greatly-exaggerated/.
17. Harvard University: "Science and religion," published in 1954, (file:///Users/janlinn/Downloads/Einstein%20Sci%20&%20Rel%20(2).pdf), p. 4.
18. Ibid.
19. (https://www.motherjones.com/mag/1997/11/toc/).
20. Ibid.
21. Ibid.
22. Ibid.
23. Oxford University Press, 2019,
24. "No God? Not so fast, say most scientists," The Catholic University website, November 2, 2016.
25. "What Scientists Really Believe" by Peter Lopatin (https://www.thenewatlantis.com/publications/what-scientists-believe).
26. Pew Research Center, "On the Intersection of Science and Religion," by Cary Lynne Thigpen, Courtney Johnson, and Cary Funk, August 20, 2020 (https://www.pewresearch.org/science/2020/08/26/on-the-intersection-of-science-and-religion/).
27. Jerry L. Sumney, The Bible: An Introduction, Third Edition (Minneapolis: Fortress Press, 2021, Kindle Edition, Loc 775.
28. Ibid., Loc 782.
29. Luther's Works, vol. 54, 379, Table Talk, 5017.

30. Ibid.
31. John Calvin, The Institutes of the Christian Religion, v. I [1559], tr. John Allen, Presbyterian Board of Publication and Sabbath-School Work, I.vi.2,I.vii.1,5, p. 85, source, "The Christian Quotation of the Day," Monday, August 14, 2017, Compilation Copyright, 1996-2024, by Robert McAnally Adams, Curator, with Robert Douglas, principal contributor.
32. In 1980 theologian Urban Holmes described biblical literalism as "a modern heresy—perhaps the only heresy invented in modern times."
Now deceased Episcopal Bishop John Shelby Spong did as well in his book, Biblical Literalism: A Gentle Heresy (HarperOne; Reprint edition (February 16, 2016).
33. Albert C. Outler ,"The Wesleyan Quadrilateral in Wesley,", Wesleyan Theological Journal Volume 20, Number 1, Spring, 1985, pp.7-18.
34. Richard Hofstadter, Anti-Intellectualism In American Life (Vintage Books, January 4, 2012), originally published in 1963.
35. This story is told in the play, "Beautiful: The Carole King Musical."
36. Noll, pp. 31-32.
37. David Steindl-Rast, Common Sense Spirituality (PublishDrive, October 1, 2008)pp.45-46).
38. Theologian Paul Tillich described God as the "ground of Being-itself" by which he meant that God pre-existed being and, thus, is the ground of all being in which God is manifested. It seems to me that what Tillich says suggests that when we speak of God, we should limit ourselves to divine attributes rather than saying who God is.
39. Sermon available at https://digitalcommons.unl.edu/cgi/viewcontent.cgi?article=1053&context=etas.
40. Hebrew Word Lessons (https://hebrewwordlessons.com/2018/05/13/helper-defining-the-ezer-woman/). Also see, Theology of Work (https://www.theologyofwork.org/key-topics/women-and-work-in-the-old-testament/god-created-woman-as-an-ezer-kind-of-helper-genesis-218/).
41. Steindle-Rast, p. 6.
42. David Wenham "Evangelical and liberal theology," Volume

14 - Issue 1, Themelios (https://www.thegospelcoalition.org/themelios/article/evangelical-and-liberal-theology/).
43. Leslie D. Weatherhead, The Transforming Friendship (Abingdon Press (September 1, 1990), originally published in 1936.
44. Marcus Borg, Meeting Jesus Again for the First Time (HarperOne, 1995).
45. His theological training was at Richmond Theological College in London. He also earned a PhD in psychology at the University of London.
46. Weatherhead, p.94.
47. P.111.
48. P.65.
49. Psychology Today: https://www.psychologytoday.com/us/basics/friends.
50. Diana Butler Bass, "The Holy Risk of Friendship: God befriends us; can we be friends to one another?" The Cottage, October 26, 2020 (Except from Chapter 1, Rediscovering Jesus as Friend, Teacher, Savior, Lord, Way, and Presence, HarperOne, March, 2021.
51. Ibid.
52. https://www.myjewishlearning.com/article/the-beginning-of-life-in-judaism/, a reprint from Fred Posner, Biomedical Ethics and Jewish Law (Ktav Pub & Distributors Inc (January 1, 2001).
53. In the fall of 2024 as I was finishing this book, The Widening of God's Grace: Homosexuality Within the Biblical Story by Richard B. Hays and Christopher B. Hays was released by Yale University Press. It explores in detail the non-prescriptive insights the Bible brings to the subject of homosexuality with the goal of helping evangelical (and all) Christians see gay and lesbian Christians as their sisters and brothers in the faith without equivocation. It is a must read, not least because of the knowledge and wisdom this father and son scholarly team bring to how to read the Bible. The authors make serious study of scripture accessible to non-scholars.
54. "There is no 'gay gene.' There is no gay-gene-there-is-no-straight-gene-sexuality-is-just-complex-study-confirmsaight

gene.' Sexuality is just complex, study confirms," by Nsikan Akpan, NPR News, August 29, 2019: https://www.pbs.org/newshour/science/
55. "Massive Study Finds No Single Genetic Cause of Same-Sex Sexual Behavior," by Sara Reardon, Sci-Am, August 29, 2019 (https://www.scientificamerican.com/article/massive-study-finds-no-single-genetic-cause-of-same-sex-sexual-behavior/).
56. Joycelyn Kaiser, "Genetics may explain up to 25% of same-sex behavior, giant analysis reveals" (Science, Aug. 29, 2019).
57. "Psychiatrists, in a Shift, Declare Homosexuality No Mental Illness," By Richard D. Lyons, Special to The New York Times (Dec. 16, 1973).
58. This is a version of a phrase attributed to philosopher George Santayana who reportedly said, "Those who cannot remember the past are condemned to repeat it."
59. (https://www.cbsnews.com/news/christianity-us-shrinking-pew-research/).
60. "New study projects that the religious identity in the US will drop below 50 percent by 2070," Christianity Today, September 13, 2022 – see the actual study: "In U.S., Decline of Christianity Continues at Rapid Pace").
61. Paul Prather, "I'll say it again: Christians, get thee to church. Now. It's important" September 5, 2024 (KY: The Lexington Herald Leader).
62. (https://www.statista.com/statistics/245485/church-membership-among-americans).
63. (Barna Research: https://christianindex.org/stories/).
64. "Louisiana governor defends Ten Commandments law," by Lauren Irwin, - 06/21/24 – The Hill (https://thehill.com/homenews/state-watch/4734128-louisiana-ten-commandments-law-jeff-landry-defends).
65. "Louisiana ranked as the worst state in US, report shows," by Tyler Eschette, May 14, 2024 (https://www.yahoo.com/news/louisiana-ranked-worst-state-us).
66. (https://newwinecollective.org/our-journal/rethinking-church-part-4-beyond-belief-1/).
67. In an article in the November 1971 issue of Psychology Today.

68. Robert Putnam, Bowling Alone: The Collapse and Revival of American Community (Simon & Schuster, 2000), p. 22. Bonding and bridging are part of what Putnam calls "social capital" that holds communal life together.
69. Ibid., p.19.
70. Ibid. pp.408-9.
71. Ibid., pp. 20-21.
72. The Henri Nouwen Society, April 23, 2024 (https://henrinouwen.org/meditations/in-prayer-we-present-our-thoughts-to-god/).
73. Graham Psychology, a group of psychological services with offices located in Melbourne, Australia (https://www.grahampsychology.com
74. Ibid.
75. "These scientists explain the power of music to spark awe," by Rob Stein, July 29, 2023 (https://www.npr.org/sections/health-shots/2023/07/29/1190374074/these-scientists-explain-the-power-of-music-to-spark-awe).
76. I don't recall whether I read this story or heard someone tell it, but I have no reason to believe it is not true since it fits what Rabbi Laufer says in the next paragraph.
77. "When It's Okay To Say Nothing" by Rabbi Sari Laufer - (https://www.myjewishlearning.com/article/when-its-ok-to-say-nothing/).
78. "What Is the Power of Regret? A Conversation with Daniel Pink, by Josh Wright, December 13, 2022 https://behaviorscientist.org/what-is-the-power-of-regret-a-conversation-with-daniel-pink/).
79. People Magazine, "Jewel on Reconciling With Her 'Abusive' Father After He Got Sober: 'I Was Determined to Heal'," by Brianne Tracy, November 19, 2020).
80. Victor Frankl, Man's Search For Meaning (Beacon, 1959)
81. Jonathon Sacks, The Dignity of Difference: How to Avoid the Clash of Civilizations, Paperback (Bloomsbury Continuum; 2nd edition, March 24, 2003).
82. Ebehardt Bethge, Dietrich Bonhoeffer: A Biography Fortress Press, Revised ed. Edition, February 18, 2000. A must read for anyone who is a student of Bonhoeffer's life and

writings.
83. Novella, p. 10.
84. Quoted in the article, "Your Brain Is Not a Video Camera" by Lawrence De Geest, May 21, 2013, Vice Media (https://www.vice.com/en/article/your-brain-is-not-a-video-camera/), from the paper, "Music Can Elicit A Vision Motion Aftereffect." by Stephen C Hedger 1, Howard C Nusbaum, Olivier Lescop, Pascal Wallisch, Berthold Hoeckner, posted on the National Lirbary of Medicine website (https://pubmed.ncbi.nlm.nih.gov/23456973/).
85. Reported in Daily Kos (https://www.dailykos.com/stories/2023/8/9/).
86. From his article, "A Christian Critique of Christian America, pp. 110-133, Vol. 30, Religion, Morality, And The Law," published By: American Society for Political and Legal Philosophy.

†

READERS GUIDE

This is no ordinary Readers Guide because of the interesting story behind how it came to be.

As the author of the book, I knew it would prove challenging for me to write questions that, ever how unintentionally, would likely show my bias in regard to the issues on which I hoped the discussions on each chapter would focus. For this reason, I asked David Digby, a trusted friend and colleague who was one of my readers, to help me with this task. We had met several years ago when I was teaching at a seminary and he was the senior minister of First Christian Church in the university town of Ames, Iowa. I was immediately struck by the ease with which he served as a pastor/theologian of that congregation. His twenty-five-year ministry there before he retired was an inspiring model of how ministers can actually provide pastoral care without neglecting the theological responsibility to engage people in thinking critically about what it means to be church and to be Christian in the modern world.

The first thing David said after agreeing to help with this Guide is that he would surmise based on the Myers-Briggs Personality Inventory that we were two very different personality types. He was exactly right. I am what Myers-Briggs identifies as an INTP, while he is an ENFJ. That means I am an introvert who thinks first and secondarily responds emotionally to situations I face. He is an extrovert who responds emotionally first before his rational side engages whatever situation he faces. One is not better than the other, simply descriptions of the way we function in life. More than that, personality types are preferences, not prisons, so introverts can extrovert and extroverts can introvert, thinking types feel and feeling types think, and so forth. His point was that he was sure our questions would likely be very different based on our personality preferences and that such differences could significantly add to the quality of the questions in the Guide.

That is precisely what I believe happened. The questions each of us wrote for the chapters clearly reflected our distinct personality types. It became clear to me as we worked through them that David's approach would be more evocative for individuals and groups whereas mine would be more provocative. What surprised me was that I preferred David's questions over mine whenever the differences were stark, the results being that the final draft of the Guide came more from him than me.

Actually, and perhaps even unconsciously, it was exactly what I had hoped would happen. I am now very confident this Guide will allow readers to respond to the material in each chapter based on their own feelings and thoughts the questions both evoke and provoke without any hidden agenda I might have inserted into the process, all because of David's good work. Thus, I think you will find this Guide a helpful aid in exploring for yourself what being a faithful skeptic can mean for a Christianity that is willing to be more honest about itself and more humble about what it says and how it says it.

Chapter 1: Getting on Track

1. What were your first impressions when you read about the concerns some Christians had about the Opening Ceremony of the 2024 Olympics in Paris (embarrassment, chagrin, delight, regret, etc.)?

2. At this juncture in your life, do you self-identify as Christian, a Christian, ex-Christian, never-Christian, or other? What has been helpful and what has been hurtful to you in your journey through the years?

3. In what ways does the fact that all church teaching comes from fallible human beings impact the way you respond to it?

Chapter 2: The Necessity of Christian Skepticism

1. Write, or tell, a brief story about a time you were either encouraged or discouraged to question something you were taught in your church. What was the impact on your understanding of Christianity in general, of church in general, and in your sense of self in particular?

2. How might cultivating healthy skepticism deepen your faith in terms of a) what you believe, b) how you read scripture, and c) how you relate to people you disagree with? What might be some downsides to Christian skepticism?

3. Given the unreliable nature of human memory, perceptions, biases and emotions, how can we trust any belief, no matter how

entrenched or cherished? How can skepticism be helpful for a thinking Christian in getting to the important questions?
Chapter 3: Skepticism and Church Teaching

1. Historically, the (white Protestant and Roman Catholic) American church has not only failed to confront the evil of racism, it has often been complicit in promulgating it. Growing up, whether you were in a church or not, what did you believe to be the church's teachings about racial relations in the United States? How has that influenced your beliefs today (positively and/or negatively)?

2. What do you think the American people have expressed regarding race and teachings they hear in church in light of the November 2024 election? For you, does it mark a failure or a success of the influence of churches in contemporary (white and POC) cultures?

3. How would a church that freely admits its humanness behave in the world in regard to race, war, poverty, the wealth gap, straight, cisgender and transgender and LBGTQ+ and nonbinary relations, environmental degradation, immigration, abortion, human rights or other hot-button issues?

Chapter 4: Making Peace with Science

1. How are the goals of Christianity and science different? How do they complement one another?

2. Dr. Linn says, "When religion fights with science, it always loses." Think of an incident when religion lost. Think of one in which it won. What, if anything, was gained in either incident?

3. Thinking of your faith, however you frame it, what is your stance regarding science—OR—if you are primarily a person of science, what is your stance regarding religion?

Chapter 5: Reading the Bible Honestly

1. Share your reactions to Dr. Linn's statement: "I think one of the missing elements in debates about the Bible today is its simple and beautiful humanness that connects modern Christians with ancient writers by making their theological perspective a basis for honest engagement rather than a matter of acceptance or rejection."

2. What does "the authority of scripture" mean in your experience and what you have learned about the Bible in the church?

3. Do you think William Lloyd Garrison's view of the Bible helps Christian skeptics read the Bible honestly? Why or why not?

Chapter 6: Remembering Who's on First

1. How do you understand the sentence in this chapter that reads, "Believing in God is an affirmation of a kind of knowing with eyes wide open to mystery"?

2. What is the "Deuteronomic ethic" (and its inversion) discussed in the chapter? Have you consciously or unconsciously thought of God this way, or have you met or known people who do?

3. If you believe in God, what are the dominant images of God that resonate most deeply in you? If you don't believe in God, note which images that some Christians find meaningful that repel you.

4. Think, or if you're in a group, talk about the kind of truth that we cannot grab and take home with us, but rather holds us when we give ourselves to it, and thereby sets us free.

Jan G. Linn

Chapter 7: Room in the Inn for Jesus

1. How did you react when you read Dr. Linn's statement, "...there was no need for Jesus to be divine to be an instrument of God..."?

2. Does the focus on Jesus being fully human such as being a friend help you identify with him more than his being God incarnate? Why or why not?

3. Jews in Jesus' time and now assert that a messiah who is also God is a theological impossibility. Why did Christians, in later centuries, come to make his divinity central to the Christian religion?

Chapter 8: Redundant Salvation

1. If your humble faithful skepticism raises questions that undermine traditional beliefs about individual salvation, do the assertions about God's saving grace being communal and unconditional provide a helpful alternative?

2. If the core of the Christian faith is not to be obedient to God's commands so we can be saved, what might that core be? What role does gratitude play?

3. What do you make of Augustine's doctrine of Original Sin and its suppositions about human beings and God's nature and the remedy required to deal with sin and evil?

Chapter 9: The Breath of Life

1. What do you make of Dr. Linn's assertion that it is useless and confusing to turn the Holy Spirit into the third person of the

trinity, writing, "The more important question is whether God is present and, if so, how, and the only way to know is through the eyes of faith. In turn, that becomes a matter of trusting God is real and present in the way you or I perceive to be the case"?

2. Can you identify a time or some time in your life when you believed yourself to have had an encounter with the Holy Spirit? What difference, if any, did it make?

3. If you were trying to explain the Holy Spirit to a skeptical person of average intelligence who had never heard of the concept, what would you lift up as important to know?

Chapter 10: The Bible and Culture Wars

1. What do you believe to be the most divisive issues in the damaging "culture wars" that are part of the American political landscape and how damaging do you think they are?

2. What are your views regarding civil rights for GLBTQ+ and non-binary Americans and a woman's right to choose whether or not to have an abortion?

3. What do you consider to be a practical way for the American people to put an end to the religious culture wars that have divided us so much? Is there anything you, as a faithful skeptic with regards to biblical teachings and interpretation, can suggest or initiate?

Chapter 11: Community Rather than Conformity

1. What do you think are the most critical reasons for the decline of the church and Christianity in today's America?

2. Does focusing on Christianity being a way of life make conformity of belief unnecessary? How so or why not? What

alternatives present themselves?

3. What does it take for community and conformity to co-exist in a state of unity? What are the hallmarks of a community that welcomes diversity? What should be said about bonding and bridging?

Chapter 12: Working Out Your Own Salvation

1. What kinds of things have you done to take responsibility for your spiritual growth and development? What things would you like to be doing to reach toward greater maturity?

2. What do you think of the idea that thinking about God's presence daily is a form of prayer?

3. Given the qualifications for being good (being as you should be, having personal integrity, being guileless and with a single-minded focus on following Jesus), how do you estimate your "goodness"?

Chapter 13: The End of Our Days

1. Do you agree that confronting the brevity of our lives highlights how precious life is? How would one confront that brevity? What benefits come from such a confrontation?

2. Does the Kilcher family story suggest how to deal with regrets all of us carry with us as we get older? If so, what is its message?

3. Can you remember instances in which you have forgiven yourself? Did you find it a difficult process? If so, does it help to remember, as Dr. Linn asserts, "forgiveness ultimately begins and ends with God, and the message Jesus gave was that God's forgiveness is 'seventy times seven,' which means 'endless. If you are worth divine forgiveness, you are worth your own"?

4. Does believing in the physical resurrection of Jesus affect your faith in God and your realization of the meaning and value of life? Why or why not?

Chapter 14: Christian Skepticism and Hope

If Hope:

—aided by skepticism does not pretend things are better than they are,
—is never based solely on evidence or circumstances,
—opens us to mystery, meaning, connections with others and joy,
—remains a fundamental hallmark of living Christian, and
—is a choice we make in adopting it as a trait

Then:

1. How does hope help you see beyond the conditions, challenges and obstacles that confront you?
2. How does hope affect your relationship with God?
3. How does believing in God affect your having hope when life is difficult?

Chapter 15: The Way Forward

1. What does your skeptical mind have to say to illustrate Dr. Linn's bold statement: "…through the centuries the church has grown closer to the world and farther from the message of Jesus"?

2. Because all Christian beliefs come from fallible human beings, is an attitude of skepticism essential for Christianity to have a future? Why or why not?

3. Based on what Dr. Linn says about humble Christianity, what

do you think it means to practice it in today's America?

Post-Script for Ministers (and Everyone in Ministry)

1. If you are reading this Postscript, you probably have received a call to some form of commissioned or ordained ministry. In your ministry setting, whether congregational, chaplaincy, specialized (youth, outdoor, education, etc.), what challenges most consume your time and attention?

2. Have you envisioned yourself as the resident theologian called to help the people you work with engage in "holy conversations" that address the big issues of the meaning of life and/or those that divide Americans? How do the questions about meaning and the divisive issues we face connect with your call?

3. The last time you wanted to quit and start selling insurance or cars or whatever, what made you stay? Did you experience a renewal and deepening of your call? Or did you stay because it's too much trouble to uproot and launch yourself into something else? How have either of those situations affected your sense of purpose and calling?